AN INTRODUCTION TO THE
STUDY OF PROGRAMMING LANGU

An Introduction to the
Study of Programming Languages

D.W. BARRON

Professor of Computer Studies
Department of Mathematics, University of Southampton

CAMBRIDGE UNIVERSITY PRESS
CAMBRIDGE
LONDON · NEW YORK · MELBOURNE

Published by the Syndics of the Cambridge University Press
The Pitt Building, Trumpington Street, Cambridge CB2 1RP
Bentley House, 200 Euston Road, London NW1 2DB
32 East 57th Street, New York, NY 10022, USA
296 Beaconsfield Parade, Middle Park, Melbourne 3206, Australia

Library of Congress catalogue card number: 76-11070

ISBN 0 521 21317 7 hard covers
ISBN 0 521 29101 1 paperback

First published 1977

Printed in Great Britain at the
University Press, Cambridge

Dedicated to the memory of Christopher Strachey, guide, philosopher and friend, who had most of the ideas first.

CONTENTS

PREFACE

There are hundreds of programming languages. How do they differ? How can we compare them? This text attempts to discuss programming languages in terms of general principles, illustrated by examples from the more popular languages. The author believes that the emphasis should be more on principles than on techniques, and the book therefore aims to introduce the basic concepts of programming language design in such a way that meaningful comparisons may be drawn between various languages.

Compiler design as such is not dealt with. Instead, language design is discussed in the context of abstract machines – a "PL/I machine", a "FORTRAN machine" etc. Since the function of a compiler is to transform from the source to run-time representation in particular pieces of hardware, the logical separation of language design and compiling technique is clearly exhibited. Sufficient attention is paid to real machines that the student can see how language design, compiler and run-time organisation mutually interact.

This is an introductory text, suitable for undergraduate computer science courses, and therefore much detail is omitted. The reader is expected to have experience in programming in at least one language, and to have a nodding acquaintance with at least one other language. It is expected that he will supplement this text by studying detailed manuals for some or all of the languages mentioned: suggestions for such reading are given in Chapter 10.

The book has its origins in a course of lectures given at the CERN Summer School held at Varenna in the summer of 1970. I am grateful to Dr G. R. McLeod for inviting me to take part in the Summer School, and for his boldness in inviting me to give a repeat performance before an audience of FORTRAN fanatics at CERN, in 1973. A later version of the lectures was given as part of a course for University staff, held at Capetown in January 1974. This was organised by the IBM Corporation, to whom I am likewise grateful. Computing is a rapidly changing subject, and the lectures evolved to keep pace with the subject. However, with the decision to commit them to print it was necessary to freeze them, and I am deeply conscious of some of the resulting omissions, notably PASCAL which receives no mention. I have attempted to make some amends for my conscious omissions in the "Suggestions for Further Reading": the unconscious omissions, of course, I can do nothing about.

I am indebted to the Universities of Glasgow, London, Newcastle and St Andrews, and to City University, for permission to reproduce examination questions. Professor Ewan Page suggested that I should write this book, and it is largely due to his gentle but persistent admonishments that it has finally seen the light of day.

Southampton, 1975   D. W. Barron

1

LANGUAGES AND PROGRAMS

And everyone will say,
As you walk your mystic way,
'If this young man expresses himself in
    terms too deep for me,
Why, what a very singularly deep young man
    this deep young man must be!'
                    W. S. Gilbert, *Patience*

Introduction

To the scientist the computer is basically a high-grade
calculating machine, whose purpose is to perform numerical
calculations. To the business man it is often just a high-grade
wages or filing clerk. We may take the view that arithmetic
and filing are the sort of drudgery that should not be inflicted
on man, because he is capable of higher things; or we may
take the more practical view that man would get the answer
wrong anyway, and therefore it is better to leave the job to a
machine. In either case, we want the machine to do something
for us, and we have to tell the machine what it is to do: this
is the purpose of programming.

Programming is the art of getting answers out of a machine,
but before we can consider this, it is necessary to consider
what sort of questions we are entitled to ask. Firstly (and
over simplifying), the answer must be some numbers and/or
some text. We cannot ask for the general solution of a
differential equation, but we can get a particular solution
subject to particular (numerical) boundary conditions. (In the
business world this difference between an analytic general
solution and the numerical particular solution does not arise.)
Thus although we cannot say to the computer

"evaluate $\int_a^b f(x)\,dx$ "

we can say

"evaluate $\quad w_i \sum_i f(x_i)$ for the given w_i and x_i "

and we can in fact choose w_i and x_i so that this sum is a
reasonable approximation to the required integral. Such a
problem formulation is the province of numerical analysis, and
when it has been done, we have in some form a description of
the number or numbers we wish to calculate. In fact we have
an algorithm for calculating the numbers. If the description is

1

implicit, e.g. "a zero of $3x^5 + 7x^2 - 4x - 1$", it must be transformed into an algorithm, i.e. a description of a finite computing process.

Exactly similar considerations apply in commercial data-processing: a problem formulation describes some numbers or text that we want, e.g.

> "a new sales ledger incorporating the week's sales into the previous ledger"

or "a list of all policy holders with five forenames"

and this description is converted into an algorithm. (The commercial data processing community call this transformation "systems analysis". We shall have more to say about the relationship of systems analysis to programming.)

The role of the programming language

When we set out to use a computer to solve a problem (or do a job), there are three stages to be followed:

(1) *Decide exactly and precisely* what is to be done. (This is often the most difficult part of the whole exercise.)

(2) Devise an algorithm: that is, a precisely defined (and finite) sequence of operations that will achieve the desired end.

(3) Express the algorithm in a form in which the computer can assimilate it.

In the world of commercial data processing, steps (1) and (2) are called systems analysis whilst step (3) is called 'programming' or 'coding'. Hence the general feeling in the commercial world that programming is a simple and inferior activity (cf. Bowden's definition of a programmer as identical with Dr Johnson's lexicographer – "a harmless drudge"). However, this distinction between analysis and programming is a false one. At the practical level the systems analyst has to communicate his solution (his algorithm) to the programmer, and to do this he needs a language to describe the algorithm. If he is debarred from using a programming language (the only satisfactory way of describing algorithms) for reasons of professional pride or status, then his communication with the programmer will be imperfect.

In the scientific world the analyst and the programmer are usually one and the same person, so the above difficulty does not arise. Thus to the scientist using a computer, the programming language is more than just a means of describing algorithms: it provides a conceptual framework in which he can think about his problems, and a notation that he can use to express his thoughts about a solution. (APL was developed as a tool for thought and exposition, and only later did it develop into a genuine programming language.)

Programming languages come in great variety, and when learning a new programming language it is sometimes best to regard it like any other foreign language: when we are learning German we do not enquire why some verbs are irregular – we complain, perhaps, then learn them by heart. It is not the purpose of this book to give detailed consideration to any particular language. Faced with a seemingly immense variation in languages we do not try to list all their properties as if cataloguing a collection of butterflies: we adopt the well-known scientific technique of abstraction. By concentrating on the similarities, and ignoring the differences for the time being, we aim to produce certain concepts that will enable us to categorise languages to a greater or lesser extent.

If we have to describe a particular language we can conveniently break down the description under several heads, e.g. kinds of data objects, rules for forming expressions, facilities for defining procedures, input–output, etc. If we applied this technique to describing a number of languages we could regard the resulting descriptions as a rectangular array in which the rows were named by the languages, and the columns were labelled by the features. In this book the description is developed "by columns", and it is assumed that the reader has access to other texts for a description of languages "by rows".

A programming language is a vehicle of communication between the programmer and his computer, and we shall consider the basic concepts that have to be conveyed in describing a computational procedure. We shall see that the design of the programming language can affect this process to a considerable degree: in a bad language it is difficult or impossible to convey certain concepts; conversely a good language should open up hitherto unappreciated concepts to the programmer, in the same way that an elegant and powerful notation (e.g. the tensor calculus) can accelerate the development of a branch of theoretical physics. We should note that any language, good or bad, may affect the way the user thinks about the solution to his problems, so that his thoughts are unconsciously confined to a restricted class of methods.

Our aim is to establish a way of talking about languages so that we can make meaningful comparisons, and try to answer the question "is x a good language for application y?". Viewed in this light, criteria that can be used to judge a language are power, relevance, simplicity and elegance. Power implies the ability to express complicated operations and concepts in a more-or-less direct manner. Relevance implies that the program is not encumbered with things that are concerned with the organisation of the computer system, though not directly relevant to the problem in hand. Simplicity requires that we can describe what is to be done concisely in a way that is easy to read and write. Elegance is defined by the Oxford English Dictionary as "refined grace or propriety; tasteful correctness; ingenious simplicity; neatness...". The reader will judge for himself as we proceed to what extent these properties are evidenced by the languages under discussion.

A language should encourage the user to write "nicely-structured" programs (we return to this point later); it should also facilitate the cultivation of a good style. We shall see later examples of language facilities which, by their capacity for opacity and or trickery, lure the user into "pornographic programming". (For example, APL tempts the programmer to try to perform as many operations as possible in one line of program – the "one-line syndrome".) However, in pursuing these aims we must never disguise the fact that the programmer is ultimately dealing with a machine. As Iverson has said of APL/360

> "..the system has been designed to minimise the distraction of the user from his problem, while not disguising the fact that he is working with a machine. The advantages that accrue from the discipline imposed by a machine are not diluted by the imposition of tasks that are essentially only clerical..".

External form

A programming language is greatly affected by the rules that govern its written form. We can instance several examples of this effect.

(i) Significance of blanks and layout

It is very common for a language designer to specify that blanks and layout (e.g. line ending, indentation) are of no significance. Bearing in mind the way in which we automatically use blanks as separators in written English, and the enormous significance of layout in normal English text, this is a truly remarkable way of going about things. Ignoring blanks does permit multi-word identifiers for variables, e.g. "position in

integer procedure fac(n);
value n; integer n;
fac := if n = 0 then 1
else n * fac(n - 1);

Figure 1. Fragment of legal Algol 60.

orbit": however, since we are pre-conditioned to blank as a word terminator the COBOL and PL/I convention of a break character is preferable, thus "position_in_orbit". Ascribing no significance to line ending leads at best to a proliferation of semi-colons, e.g.

$$a := 3.1;$$
$$b := 4.2;$$
$$c := 5.6$$

and at worst it makes the program shown in figure 1 a legal Algol program. At the other extreme, some languages (notably FORTRAN and COBOL) are designed on the assumption that the input will be from punched cards, and require items to be placed in specified fields on the line, which leads to difficulty when using a time-sharing terminal, for example.

(ii) Reserved words

Some languages reserve to themselves words like GOTO that are significant to the syntax. COBOL is the worst offender, having over three hundred words that the programmer must not use for his own purposes. At the other extreme, FORTRAN and PL/I have no reserved words: the burden is placed on the compiler, where it properly belongs. Thus in FORTRAN it is legitimate to use DO, REAL, FORMAT etc. as variable names (though exploitation of this facility is not to be recommended – it makes programs obscure and needlessly difficult to read). The designers of Algol 60 hit upon the happy idea of reserving words by using a different typeface (bold type in printed material). For machine input they suggested underlining, but since there are few input devices that can produce underlining it is usually necessary to resort to the ugly expedient of using quotes, e.g.

'REAL' ALPHA; 'INTEGER' I;

If input devices (and output devices) with upper and lower case alphabets are available, the ALGOL 68–R convention of using upper case for system words and lower case for programmer's names is attractive, e.g.

IF x < y THEN z := x;

(iii) Comments

Comments addressed to the human reader and ignored by the compiler are essential. FORTRAN insists that comments occupy a line to themselves (with C in the first column) which severely restricts their usefulness. Much to be preferred is the PL/I technique of comment brackets that allows comments to

6

be interspersed wherever they are meaningful, e.g.

```
IF X /*THE DISPLACEMENT*/ > 3.754
    THEN CALL ALARM /*BECAUSE IT IS PAST
    THE SAFE LIMIT */;
```

Algol 68 uses a similar principle using identical forms for the opening and closing "bracket" (**comment** or **co** or **c**). ALGOL 60 is more restrictive, allowing comments after a begin or an end, or anywhere that a semi-colon can occur. The danger of a comment facility is that if the comment is not correctly terminated a whole section of program can be ignored: for this reason some designers treat end-of-line as a comment delimiter.

(iv) Literal strings

One of the more remarkable survivals from the early days of FORTRAN is the notation for Hollerith strings

31HWHICH REQUIRE AN EXPLICIT COUNT

This construction is error-prone, decreases legibility, and is actually more trouble to compile than a string

'DELIMITED BY QUOTES'

The only snag to using quotes is the problem of including a quote in a string. Various expedients are used: only SNOBOL4 takes the sensible way out. In that language single or double quotes can be used, the closing quotes being of the same variety as the quotes that opened the string, e.g.

"IT'S POSSIBLE TO HAVE A QUOTE IN A STRING"

or "STRINGS 'CAN BE NESTED "INDEFINITELY IN THIS WAY" AS YOU CAN' SEE"

(v) Character set

Languages are severely restricted by the character set available on most computer input devices, most commonly the 64-character punched card set. However, there is no excuse for FORTRAN's insistence that .GT. be used for "greater than" when the available character set includes the symbol '>'.

Structured programming

A recent advance in programming has been the general recognition of the virtues of structured programs, and a desirable feature of a language is that it should assist the programmer to produce programs that are "nicely structured", in the sense that the structure of the program reflects directly the structure of the problem, and perspicuous, in the sense that they can be read rather like a mathematical textbook. In seeking nicely-structured programs we are not pursuing elegance for its own sake. Such programs will be easier to follow: they are less likely to contain errors, and the errors that they contain will be easier to find. Conversely, if the language forces us into the use of devious methods to achieve the ends we desire, the program will be more prone to error and harder to debug.

One of the characteristics of nicely-structured programs is that they shun the use of **goto**'s and labels, since the use of **goto** is one of the major contributory factors towards making programs difficult to follow. We take up this point again when we discuss control structures in Chapter 3. The other important aspect of structured programs is that they are made up of modules whose structure and relationship model the problem. A major factor in making this possible is the use of procedures, as discussed in Chapter 4.

We note in parenthesis that flowcharting, the unproductive draughtsmanship so beloved by some practitioners of the programming art, is made redundant by structured programming. The flow chart of a nicely structured program is trivially simple, and more insight can be obtained by actually reading the code than by studying the flowchart.

Procedures and data

A language provides a conceptual framework in two ways. First there are the kinds of operation that can be carried out: second there are the types of data item and arrangements of data items that can be processed. These two aspects are not usually very clearly separated in scientific languages, whereas in COBOL the program is clearly separated into a procedure division and a data division. Familiar scientific languages usually operate on nothing more complicated than an array, though we shall later encounter languages that cater for more elaborately structured data.

Program correctness

One of the major problems in computing is knowing whether the answers are correct. Whilst the advent of high level languages has transformed programming from an esoteric art to a skill that can be acquired by anyone of modest intelligence, it cannot be denied that in making it easy to obtain *some* results from a machine, the over-riding importance of ensuring that they are the *correct* results tends to have been overlooked. A good language will therefore to a greater or lesser extent prevent a user from making mistakes. A weaker requirement (almost as useful, and much more easily achieved) is that the language should make it difficult to make mistakes that cannot be detected at compile time. An obvious example is the requirement (e.g. in Algol 60) that all variables be declared before they are used. This removes mis-spelling of names from the class of undetected mistakes.

Compiling and interpreting

A program is essentially an algorithm cast in a form suitable for automatic execution. The execution can take two forms. We can scan the text and perform the indicated operations directly: this is called interpretation. Alternatively we can generate an equivalent program in another language: if this is the machine code of the target machine it can be executed directly by the hardware. This process is called compiling.

In general interpretation is slower and less efficient than compiling. If an operation is only to be performed once there is little to choose, but as soon as an operation is repeated several times e.g. in a loop, compiling gains because the over-heads of analysis are incurred only once. However, the balance is also affected by the nature of the language. For example, if operand types are not declared explicitly then much of the analysis must necessarily be done at run-time, and the advantage of compiling is that much less. These questions are really outside the scope of this book, and we shall often use the phrase "evaluation of the program text" to denote the operation of finding out what the text means, without specifying whether it is to be compiled or interpreted.

Varieties of programming language

Languages can be categorised in various ways. Whilst we shall later develop ways of categorising languages more precisely, it is perhaps worth making some rather loose distinctions now.

Commercial vs Scientific

"Commercial" languages emphasise handling of files and alpha-numeric data, whereas "scientific" languages emphasise the manipulation of numeric data.

Interactive vs Batch

"Interactive" languages provide facilities which assume that the programmer will be on hand during compiling and execution, and may wish to make corrections and/or changes at either stage. "Batch" languages make no such provision.

Imperative vs Functional

The languages with which we are familiar are mainly imperative, that is they are composed of a sequence of imperative commands that perform the desired operations. In contrast there are languages (LISP is the prime example) in which the fundamental operation is the evaluation of a function, so that the characteristic form of a program is

results = f (input values)

Markov languages

Another category is that of Markov languages (e.g. SNOBOL). Here the basic operation is to look for a pattern, make a specified substitution, and choose a successor statement on the outcome of the match. Markov languages have some claim to be more "fundamental" than others, since it is arguable that all algorithms can be reduced (ultimately) to Markov sequences.

"Real Time" languages

The designation "real-time" applied to a language is a puzzling one. It is evidently meant to imply that the language is suitable for programming real-time applications, but in practice it often seems that the only features included for this purpose are some bit-manipulation operations and the ability to use pointers. If the term "real-time language" has any significance, it should pertain to a language in which it is possible to specify a number of autonomous procedures, to activate them in response to interrupts, and to synchronise them as required. There is a considerable overlap here with the operating system, which may explain why general-purpose machine-independent languages are not generally available (despite the contrary claims of the advocates of CORAL 66).

In the subsequent development we shall introduce examples from a variety of languages. Anyone with pretensions to authority in this field should have at least a reading knowledge of a number of languages. As Meek has written,
"...once a person becomes a programmer he should become a good programmer, part of being a good programmer is a continuing desire to become a better programmer, and a good way of becoming a better programmer is to become a

good programming linguist, fluent in several tongues. A case could certainly be made out that positive harm has been done and is being done by moderately good programmers becoming too complacent and/or conservative, and thinking the language they have is, in all senses, the last word."

(A correspondent in "Computerworld" put it more strongly – "...until all COBOL-only and FORTRAN-only programmers are eliminated there is no chance for the rest of us to achieve professional status.")

2

OBJECTS, NAMES AND VALUES

"...it's useful to the people that name them, I suppose.
If not, why do things have names at all?"
    Lewis Carroll: *Through the Looking Glass*

Names and references

Programs operate on data objects that are identified by names. Terminology here is extremely lax, and if we are not careful we can get into deep water when we try to describe some of the more sophisticated operations provided in some languages. For example, we say

"X has the value 2.4"

when we really mean

"X is the name of a place where the quantity 2.4 is presently stored".

Here we are making clear the distinction between the container and the thing contained. Or we may say

"X has the value π"

when we really mean

"X is the name of a place where there is presently stored the number called π".

(In Lewis Carroll's *Through the Looking Glass*, the White Knight explained the difference between

(i) the song
(ii) what the song is called
(iii) the name of the song
(iv) what the name is called.

In our case

(i) the number is 3.1415926535.....
(ii) the number is called π
(iii) the name of the number is some physical core address

and   (iv) the name is called X.)

The confusion between the container and the object contained arises because we use the same name for both. Thus in the FORTRAN statement

$$I = I + 1$$

the I occurring on the left is identifying the container, and on the right it is standing for the value contained. We can say that on the left we have a **reference** and on the right we have a **value**. A more complicated situation is exemplified by the statement

$$A(I + 1) = A(I + 2) + B$$

Although the left-hand side of the assignment must specify a place to store a value, in this case specifying a place involves a computation, as does obtaining a value in the similar term on the right-hand side.

To resolve the ambiguity we need to formalise and elaborate our concept of a variable. A variable has associated with it two objects:

> a *reference*, which identifies an area in the store, and a *value*, which is a storable object to be manipulated by the program.

A variable is identified by a *name*, and the relationship between name, reference and value is shown in the diagram.

name   reference   value

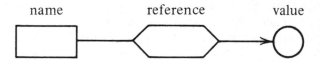

We can now see how the ambiguity in the use of names in statements like I = I + 1 is resolved. The I on the left-hand side stands for the reference (because it is defining a place to put something), whilst the I on the right stands for the value (since it is needed in a computation). The mnemonic terms L-value and R-value are sometimes used instead of reference and value, but the latter form is to be preferred since it leaves open the possibility of using references in contexts other than assignment (e.g. passing arguments to a procedure). It also avoids confusion when dealing with languages that write assignments back-to-front, e.g. $I + 1 \rightarrow I$ instead of $I = I + 1$.

In a sense the reference is a sort of name, since it identifies a value. However, it is a hidden name accessible only to the compiler.* In most languages the concept of the reference does not appear explicitly, though it is a powerful expository tool. However, in ALGOL 68 references can be manipulated, and can be the values of other variables. In such a language the clear separation of the unchanging name and the possibly changing reference makes it possible to speak meaningfully of "variables whose values are names of other variables".

A reference is a pointer (hence the arrow in the diagram), and we can postulate a unique-valued function "contents of" to transform a reference into a value. The inverse mapping is less useful since it may not be unique: for example:

name   reference   value

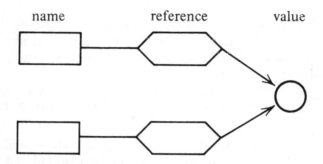

An immediate and useful extension of the reference concept is that an *expression* may yield a reference instead of a value. The usual process of evaluating an expression is to replace all the variable names by the associated values, and perform the operations indicated. To be precise, we say that this is evaluation in *R-mode*. There is the possibility of evaluating in *L-mode* by substituting references for names instead of values. This is not generally possible because there are not many operators that take references as operands. Thus it is meaningless to evaluate A + B in L-mode. But consider the ALGOL 60 expression

      if *b* **then** *x* **else** *y*

If values are substituted for *x* and *y* this yields a value, but if references are substituted, it yields a reference. This mode of evaluation would be used in the following statement (not legal in ALGOL 60!):

      (**if** *b* **then** *x* **else** *y*) := *z* ;

---

* Readers familiar with Tolkien's *The Lord of the Rings* will recall that in Middle-Earth each dwarf has his own secret and inner name, his 'true' name, never revealed to anyone of alien race.

or even

$$(\text{if } b1 \text{ then } x \text{ else } y) := (\text{if } b2 \text{ then } w \text{ else } z);$$

This latter statement is much more perspicuous than the equivalent form

```
begin
z1 := if b2 then w else z;
if b1 then x := z1 else y := z1;
end
```

since it is clearly an assignment, and we can concentrate attention separately on what is being assigned and where it is being put.

We can now give a precise interpretation of array references. We first note that when we write something like $A(I + 1)$ there is an implied operation, that of subscripting. $A(I + 1)$ is a syntactic abbreviation for $A \downarrow (I + 1)$ where $\downarrow$ is the subscripting operator. The operator takes two operands, a reference (the array name) and a value (the index) and produces *another* reference (the location of the particular element). Consider again the statement

$$A(I + 1) = A(I + 2) + B$$

On the left-hand side we have $A \downarrow (I + 1)$ which yields a reference as required. On the right-hand side evaluation of $A \downarrow (I + 2)$ will yield a reference, and the required value is obtained by using the "contents of" operator which takes the reference and delivers the corresponding value. Looking at this in a slightly different way, we can say that $A \downarrow (I + 2)$ yields a reference but since it is an operand of '+', which requires a value, we immediately use the "contents" operator. This is a more general view, which, as will be seen later, extends naturally to more complex situations.

Evaluation of an expression can now be described as follows. The expression is made up of names, constants and operators. (Constants are objects, which in effect have only a value.) Names are initially replaced by references. The operators are then applied in the appropriate sequence, and if an operator which requires a value as operand finds itself provided with a reference the "contents" operator is invoked. For example, consider the expression

$$(\text{if } b \text{ then } x \text{ else } y) + z$$

Initially the references associated with b, x, y and z are substituted: let these be \$1, \$2, \$3, \$4 respectively. The first operator to be evaluated is **if**. This requires a value for its first operand, so we take Contents($1). The **if** can now be evaluated yielding $2 or $3. The next operator to be dealt with is '+': this requires values so we must use the "contents" operator on $2 or $3 as appropriate and ,$4. The net result is a value, since 'plus' always yields a value. This is an example of what ALGOL 68 calls de-referencing (more examples later). In some languages (e.g. BLISS), names always stand for references and the "contents of" operation is explicit. PL/I provides the operation "address of": this is mainly used in conjunction with pointer manipulation (see Chapter 5).

References and addresses

It may seem that a reference is nothing more than an address. This is not so: a reference describes an area of store large enough to hold the object being stored, and may correspond to a whole range of physical store addresses. Moreover, the mapping of references on to physical addresses may vary as the program runs if a dynamic storage allocation scheme is in use. Essentially, the reference is a pointer to an area of store: the area pointed to may vary, but the pointer will always be found in the same position. In block-structured languages the name/reference correspondence may also change, since the same name may be used for different objects at different times as the program runs. (Block structure is discussed in more detail below.)

It should be noted that "address" calculations in a high level language are only possible if the address space is regarded as an ordering of references. In ALGOL 60, if a number of variables are declared simultaneously, e.g. **real** x, y, z, there is no requirement that x, y and z should occupy adjacent (or even related) areas of store, so that no address calculations are possible. (This is an important point if a high level language is to be used for system development work.)

Data Attributes

Thus far we have been mainly concerned with the naming of objects, and the examples used have involved mainly numeric quantities. However, the value is defined as a *storable object* and is thus a much more general thing than a number. Other storable objects include truth values, character strings, procedures (pieces of program) and references. Allowing procedure bodies as values allows us to perform a number of useful manipulations. Allowing references means that we can have a 'variable' whose 'value' is the identity of another variable

16

(i.e. a pointer). This brings the concept of indirect addressing into high-level languages, and is the key to "list processing" and similar activities in high level languages.

Given a value, we define what sort of object it is by specifying its *attributes*. The most important attribute is *class* e.g. numeric, truth value, procedure, reference, etc. In some cases, particularly numeric items, further attributes are required, to define the *representation*. The attributes may be regarded as part of the reference, which thus comprises an identification of an area of store and information as to how to interpret what we find there, or as part of the value. (Putting this another way we can say that the reference defines an area of store and tells us what sort of object we can put there, or that it just defines an area of store, and we find out by looking what can be stored there.) We can classify languages according to the way attributes are treated. In an *L-typed* language the attributes are part of the reference: in an *R-typed* language they are part of the value. L-typed languages allow more rigorous checking at compile time: R-typed languages allow more flexibility at run-time and are usually more suited to interactive, conversational working.

The class of an object determines the kind of operations that can be carried out on it. In evaluating an expression, having obtained the operands for an operator we must check the class to make sure that the operation is a valid one, e.g. '+' is only valid if both operands are of numeric class.

The results of an arithmetic operation can be defined without knowing the representation of the numbers. Thus we can say

$$2 + 2 = 4$$
$$\text{or} \quad II + II = IV$$

and both these describe the same abstract calculation. There is an abstract concept "two" which can be represented on paper as 2 or II. However, given the sum

$$IX + 5 =$$

we would have to apply a *representation conversion* to either the IX or the 5, depending on the representation required for the result. (Note particularly that IX ɪ 5 makes sense, whereas 4 + **false** does not, since one of the operands of + is of the wrong class in the second case.) Representation is important when we come to mechanise computation, since it determines the machine operations required and also the accuracy that we can expect in the result. For example, we can avoid the errors arising from decimal to binary conversion if BCD arithmetic is available. Ironically, this is usually used only for integer arithmetic, where the errors do not arise. The task of the compiler is made more complicated by the fact that a single symbol may be used to define an operation although there are several possible representations of the operands. Thus in the expression x > y, the operation to be carried out is entirely different depending as x, y are represented in fixed-point or floating-point. Moreover, if both operands do not have the same representation, then some conversion has to be carried out. The extent to which representation conversions are automatic (as opposed to being explicitly programmed) is an important decision in the design of a language, and is discussed later when we consider evaluation of expressions.

Most scientific languages distinguish only two representations for numeric quantities – integer and real, corresponding to fixed and floating point hardware. It is implicitly assumed that the internal representation is invariant and no provision is made for the fact that a machine like the System/370 can do arithmetic on numbers either in binary or in character form.

The attributes of an object determine its *type* (or *mode*). They may be *manifest* i.e. explicitly specified, or *latent* i.e. deducible by examination. (For example, 3.14159 is evidently numeric and non-integer.) An indirect way of defining attributes is by specifying the way in which a piece of data is to be used. Thus in COBOL we can include in the description of a data object

$$\text{USAGE IS} \begin{cases} \text{COMPUTATIONAL} \\ \text{DISPLAY} \end{cases}$$

This leaves it open for the language implementation to choose the most appropriate representation for the particular hardware being used. (Thus an integer described as COMPUTATIONAL might well be held in binary representation for efficiency in computation.)

Scientific languages do not always make provision for varying the precision with which variables are stored. FORTRAN offers only single-length INTEGER arithmetic, but allows DOUBLEPRECISION as an option in place of REAL. ALGOL 60 does not offer any choice of precision. PL/I on the other hand appears to allow complete freedom in the choice of precision, though in fact if a variable has the FLOAT attribute it will be represented in one of the two (or possibly three) available floating-point precisions, whatever the program says. ALGOL 68 recognises the facts of multi-length working and allows precision to be extended a word at a time by the prefix

long. Thus we have, for example, **long real** (double-length floating), **long long int** (triple precision integer), etc.

A note on logical (Boolean) variables

The concepts of class and representation are illuminated by a consideration of the way in which logical variables are treated in different languages. These variables can take only two possible values, and are used to record truth values. Boolean values can be formed as the result of a relational operator ($>$, $<$, $=$, $\neq$, etc.) operating on two numerical values, and expressions involving such values can be constructed using the operators and, or, etc. In ALGOL 60 the two possible values are denoted by the symbols **true** and **false** (the FORTRAN convention is .TRUE. and .FALSE.) and it is not possible to mix Boolean values and numeric values in an expression since they belong to different classes. (Thus an expression like $3 +$ **true** is meaningless, and illegal.) However, other languages provide an explicit correspondence between Booleans and numbers. Thus in PL/I **false** is any bit-string that contains all zero bits (or is an empty string), and **true** is a bit string that contains at least one non-zero bit. (Comparison operators yield one-bit strings.) Similarly, in POP-2 any non-zero value is treated as "true" in a Boolean context, zero denoting "false". Thus if b is a one-bit string, the PL/I construction

$$b * x + (\neg b) * y$$

is equivalent to the Algol 60 conditional expression

    if b **then** x **else** y

(APL uses a similar method to provide conditional expressions.) It can be argued that if in a language true and false are represented by one and zero respectively then it is bad practice to permit mixing of classes (as in $3 +$ **true**) since the value of such an expression depends on what is really an accident of representation. Such representation-conversion should be explicit, thus $3 + $ num(**true**). However, it is possible to define the logical operations as numerical functions whose domain and range both consist only of the integers 0 and 1, and to define the relational operators as functions that map pairs of numbers on to the integers 0 and 1. It is then quite legitimate to include "truth values" in arithmetic expressions, since there is no conflict of class. This is the way APL treats logical variables and is essentially the PL/I approach. It leads to difficulties, however. Consider an expression such as $a < b < c$. PL/I will parse this as $(a < b) < c$, and when evaluated this reduces to 1<c or 0<c, according as the relation a<b is true or false. Thus if c>1 the expression will always yield the value **true**, whatever the values of a and b. Thus PL/I will yield true for 7<8<9 and for 9<8<7. This will cause great confusion to the user who thinks that he is evaluating (a<b)∧(b<c). Similar confusion can arise in APL. If logical variables were regarded as distinct from numeric variables, an expression like a<b<c with a, b, c all numeric could be detected as incorrect at compile time.

Declarations

In all but the simplest languages programmers are allowed to introduce their own names for variables. (BASIC is an example of a language with a fixed repertoire of names.) In FORTRAN a new variable can be implicitly introduced by the first use of a new name, but in almost all other languages it is necessary to introduce new variables by means of a class of statements called **declarations**.

In an R-typed language the sole function of a declaration is to introduce a new name to the system, thus in POP-2 we would write

VARS X Y Z;

to introduce the names X, Y, Z. Such a declaration might seem to be superfluous, but it imposes a certain discipline on the programmer, and protects him against the consequences of an inadvertent mis-spelling of a name.

In an L-typed language the declaration also serves to specify (either explicitly or by implication) the attributes of the data object associated with the name. This puts a further discipline on the programmer, and makes it possible to carry out a large amount of consistency checking during the compiling phase. Full checking is only possible if all declarations are explicit. The FORTRAN rules for determining type from the initial letter of the name do not protect against mis-spelling.

The ALGOL 60 declaration "**real** x" is usually described as "introducing a new variable x, of type **real**". A variable is an association of name, reference and value, so the above declaration can more precisely be defined as "associate the name x with a reference to a **real** value": thus

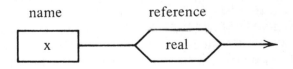

Note that the declaration actually causes some operations to be carried out. The FORTRAN programmer regards declarations as static objects whose purpose is to convey information to the compiler (hence the name "non-executable statements"), but this reflects the fact that in FORTRAN all storage allocation is usually done prior to execution of the program. More sophisticated languages use a dynamic storage allocation system, in which context the declaration becomes something to be obeyed at run-time. In fact, in ALGOL 68 the declaration **real** x; is a syntactic abbreviation for the construction **ref real** x = **loc real**; . This shows explicitly that x is a reference to a **real** value; the construction '**loc real**' is a local generator which actually acquires the space to be associated with the reference attached to the name x. (Thus we might say that the 'value' of the reference is the 'address' of the space produced by the generator.) The **loc** indicates that this is local space that will be relinquished later in the program: the range over which it exists is the scope of x (see below). Generators will appear again in Chapters 4 and 5 when we discuss functions and structures.

The above explanation of the declaration is incomplete: since the store must contain something, there is an implicit assignment x := rubbish. The diagram becomes

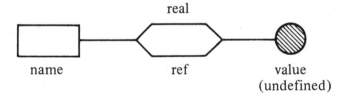

where we have introduced the convention that shading denotes an undefined value. It is not strictly necessary for a declaration to be dealt with this way: the reference could have been left not filled in, thus:

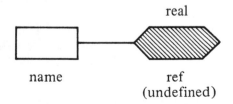

This would be the case with a PL/I variable using ALLOCATED storage. (An explicit ALLOCATE command must be used to fill in the reference before the variable is used for the first time.)

In the declaration **real** x, the class is explicit, and the representation is implicit; probably the only possible representation of a real, though it might be a particular representation assumed by default. In PL/I the declaration specifies the attributes in much more detail, e.g.

DECLARE A REAL FIXED DECIMAL (5)
DECLARE B REAL DECIMAL FLOAT (6)

Initialised declarations

An obvious extension to the declaration structure outlined above is to specify the initial value in the declaration. Thus in PL/I we can add the qualifier INITIAL (...) to a declaration, and in ALGOL 68 we can write

real x := 4.735

which is equivalent to the combination

(**real** x; x := 4.735)

(The FORTRAN DATA statement is a form of initialised declaration. However it is obeyed only once, at compile time, whereas the initialisation specified in a PL/I or ALGOL 68 declaration takes place every time the declaration is encountered in the dynamic flow of the program.)

In principle there is no reason why the initial value should not be specified as an expression, e.g.

real x := ($y*$ 3.1415926536)/180;

With such an initialised declaration the attributes of the variable could be deduced from the right-hand side, thus in CPL it is permitted to write

let x := 3.14159;

This is another example of latent (as compared with manifest) information.

It is often convenient in programs to use a name for a numerical constant (e.g. Pi for the constant 3.14159....). The declaration

real Pi := 3.1415926536;

allows this, but leaves it open to the unwary programmer to accidentally redefine the value of Pi somewhere in his program. ALGOL 68 permits the definition of constants thus:

real x = 3.1415926536;

Although this looks like a declaration, it is essentially different since it defines an equivalence, saying that any occurrence of *x* is to be replaced by the symbol string on the right of the equals. Any attempt to redefine *x* will, by this substitution, result in an assignment with a constant on the left-hand side which is clearly absurd. (There is a close analogy here with a macro without parameters. However, it is more than a simple textual substitution, since class and representation information are associated with the value.) We can regard this declaration as producing a disembodied R-value, associated with the name but not accessible by a "contents of" operation: pictorially

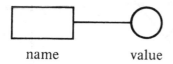

as opposed to

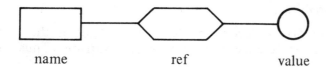

In most languages, a declaration introduces a name and acquires a new piece of store. This need not be so however. In FORTRAN the EQUIVALENCE statement allows several names to be associated with the same area of store, and this idea can be generalised as follows. We introduce a new notation, thus

real *variable* $\simeq$ *expression*

which is interpreted as follows: evaluate the expression in L-mode and associate the resulting reference with the name 'variable'. Thus if we have a 2-dimensional array A, then

real $z \simeq A\,[i, j]$

makes *z* a name for the element $A\,[i,j]$, a particular element, defined by the values of *i* and *j* when this declaration is obeyed. (Thus subsequent changes to *i* and *j* will not change

23

the meaning of z.) Pictorially, we get a situation thus:

real y := 2.0

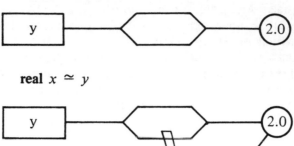

real $x \simeq y$

We consider this type of declaration further in the next section.

Reference variables

One of the important developments in ALGOL 68 is the ability to have a reference as the value of a variable. Thus we can declare

ref real xx;

meaning that xx is a reference to a place where a reference to a **real** can be stored. Thus if we write

real x := 2.0; **ref real** xx;
. . .
xx := x

we get the situation

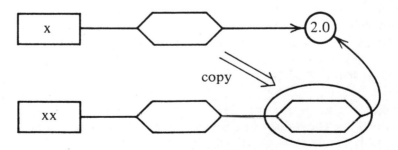

(The arrow ⇒ signifies the copying that takes place on assignment.)

The initialisation denoted above by the ≃ symbol can be achieved in the following way. Suppose we have the declarations

> real x := 2.0,
> **real** y := x;

then the effect is as follows:

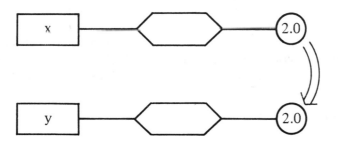

In contrast,

> **real** x := 2.0;
> **ref real** y := x;

gives rise to:

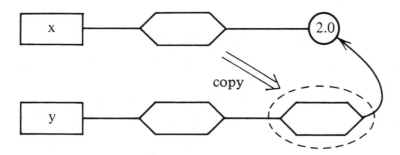

It is important to appreciate the difference between these two situations. In ALGOL indefinite chains of "refs" are permitted, e.g.

> **ref ref ref real** z;

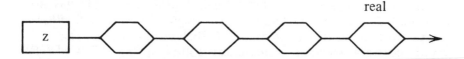

Scopes

A further function of declarations can be to specify the scope (or extent) of a name; that is, the range of the program over which a name is valid. Thus in FORTRAN, a name is local to a program unit (subroutine or function) unless it is declared to be in a COMMON block. In more sophisticated languages the association between a name and a reference is not necessarily maintained throughout the program. The most common pattern is a nested block structure. A block consists of a section of program preceded by declarations, and the convention is that a name declared at the head of the block has a *scope* or *extent* (i.e. an association with the new reference) that lasts throughout the block and any enclosed blocks, unless a variable of the same name is declared in an inner block. For example, suppose we have

> **begin real** x, y, z;
>   . . .
>   . . .
> **begin real** x;
>   . . .
>   . . .
> **end**
>   . . .
>   . . .
> **end**

The declaration of x at the head of the inner block temporarily supersedes the meaning (L-value) associated with x; this old association is re-established at the end of the inner block. We say that there is a "hole in the extent" of the first x, or that it is "occluded". Some languages (e.g. POP-2) provide an explicit way of breaking the association between a name and a reference, so freeing the name for re-use. In ALGOL 68 the simple idea of blocks delimited by **begin** and **end** is refined somewhat. The scope of a declaration extends from the closest opening-context symbol to the matching closing-context symbol. Thus **begin...end** is included as one possibility, but in addition **if...fi, then...else** and **else...fi** are some of the other scope delimiters.

If, as in PL/I, the FORTRAN rules for default declaration based on initial letter are combined with block structure, difficulties can arise. The problem is that if a variable has no explicit declaration its scope is not explicitly delimited. PL/I says that the scope of an implicit declaration is as if the variable were declared immediately following the PROCEDURE statement of the external procedure in which the name is used. Thus in effect an implicit declaration extends throughout a procedure except in inner blocks where a variable of the same name is explicitly declared. This trap is particularly likely to catch the unwary programmer who does not declare his loop control variables. For example, consider the following outline PL/I program

```
CATCH:  PROCEDURE OPTIONS (MAIN)
           .
           .
           .
    B:    BEGIN
             DO I = 1 TO 20 BY 2
             . . .
             C:   BEGIN
                    I = . . .
                    .
                    .
                    .
                  END C
             . . . . .
           END B
    END CATCH
```

The programmer may think that he has got two different I's for the two loops, whereas the first occurrence of I in block B will declare it globally, and as a result his repetition loops will become hopelessly entangled. To obtain the desired effect each BEGIN should be followed by a declaration of I, e.g. DECLARE I FIXED BINARY (15).

When reference variables are used, further difficulties may occur. For example, compare the following situations

```
(a)  begin
       real x;
       . . . .
         begin ref real xx;
         . . . .
         xx := x
         . . . .
         end;
       . . . .
     end
```

(b) **begin**
    ref real xx;

    . . . .

      begin real x;

      . . . .

      $xx := x$;

      . . . .

      end;

   L: . . .

  end

Case (a) is quite straightforward. But in case (b), in the inner block we assign as the value of xx a reference to a variable x which does not exist outside the inner block. What is the value of xx at the point labelled L?

Store allocation

A reference is a pointer to a place where something can be stored. We have so far assumed (implicitly) that an infinite supply of storage cells is available. Any practical realisation of a programming language must operate using a bounded number of storage cells and the strategy of allocating storage cells for references is an important part of the compiling process. This strategy can be influenced (or even dictated) by the language design. Basically we distinguish two allocation strategies: *static* and *dynamic*. The terms are self-explanatory: in static allocation the relation between references and storage cells remains the same throughout the running of the program: dynamic allocation means that the relation between references and storage cells changes as the program runs. Static allocation implies that the allocation can be done *before* the program starts running, i.e. at compile time (or linkage-edit time), which in turn means that there are no run-time overheads adding to the execution time of the program. However, the price paid for this efficiency is high in terms of the constraints imposed on the language in order to achieve the static relationship between references and storage cells. Essentially it means that either all variables have global scope, as in BASIC, or the FORTRAN rules. (These are that the scope is either one program unit (subroutine or function), or a number of program units as specified by declarations of COMMON blocks.) Static allocation also implies that all array sizes are fixed at compile time and rules out the possibility of recursive procedures. (Note that static allocation is not, as is commonly believed, necessary for FORTRAN, though it is sufficient.)

If dynamic allocation is used, then declarations are "obeyed" as they are encountered during the execution of a program. Each time a reference is created a new storage cell is taken. Since the number of storage cells is bounded, there must evidently be some means of recovering the storage used for references that have ceased to exist. An advantage of the commonly used nested block structure is that cells are discarded in the reverse order to that in which they were obtained, so that the run-time storage can be based on a simple stack structure. Once reference variables are introduced it may no longer be possible to use a simple stack since the last-in-first-out rule may no longer apply. An advantage of stack based storage is that it allows array sizes to be dynamically determined, thus we can write in ALGOL 60

```
begin   integer n;
        . . . .
        n:=. . . .
        begin real array A [1:n, 1:n] ;
        . . . .

        . . . .
        end;
 . . . .
 end
```

However, this only works as long as the array size remains fixed within the scope of the array name (i.e. the block) as is the case in ALGOL 60 and PL/I. When we manipulate text strings, we have arrays that can change size from statement to statement, and a more elaborate storage allocation strategy is required. ALGOL 68 gets round the difficulty very neatly by using stack-based storage wherever possible, and using a separate dynamically administered area called the heap for storage of variable length items and other items that do not conform to the last-in-first-out rule. A particular attraction of this approach is that if the programmer does not use any of the facilities that require heap storage he does not incur the space and time penalties of the heap storage organisation routines (in particular the garbage collector). In PL/I the programmer can specify storage class as an attribute for each variable as it is declared. The classes are STATIC, i.e. conventional FORTRAN type storage; AUTOMATIC – conventional ALGOL-type stack storage; and CONTROLLED. A CONTROLLED variable is not allocated any store until an explicit ALLOCATE command is issued: it then remains available until released by a FREE command. Note that there is no garbage collector, so the programmer must explicitly free

storage for re-use. This is an unhappy compromise. STATIC
allocation is often used for arrays in PL/I. It can be argued
that if the size of an array is constant then there is no point
in involving the overhead of making its storage AUTOMATIC,
though this is an argument of doubtful validity. More valid
arguments for STATIC storage will become apparent when we
discuss procedures in Chapter 4. (It gives equivalents to
FORTRAN COMMON storage and ALGOL 60 **own** variables.)

In a language with a nested block structure, the dynamic
relationship of names, references, values and storage locations
becomes quite complex. For example, consider the following
ALGOL 60 procedure:

> **procedure** *fred*(*a, b*) ;
> . . . . . .
> **begin real** *x*;
> L1: . . .
> . . . .
> > **begin integer array** *x* [1 : 100] ;
> > L2: . . . .
> > . . .
> > **end**;
> . . . . .
> **end**

At L1 the name *x* is associated with a reference which points
to an area of store that will hold a real variable, whilst at L2,
x is associated with a different reference, this time to an area
large enough to hold an array of 100 integers. Both of these
references will point to areas on the stack, defined relative to
the stack pointer on entry to the procedure. So each time the
procedure is called it is likely that different physical store
addresses will be involved.

A nested block structure has many attractions. It allows the
compiler to determine the essential environment for each block,
and by allowing the programmer to declare items at the places
where they are required it encourages the production of
programs that display a high degree of locality. This is
particularly important in the context of paged-store machines:
a program with good locality tends to have a small working
set and therefore performs well in a paged environment.

An aspect of block structure that is often overlooked is that
it gives an elegant way of providing default definitions. Thus a
program can be surrounded by an outer block that contains
definitions of useful procedures (e.g. post-mortem diagnostics)

and variables (e.g. standard I/O channel assignments). If the programmer declares objects of the same name his definitions will take precedence by the normal rules of block structure, and those standard variables that he does not declare explicitly will retain their default declarations from the outer block.

The subject of scope has further ramifications in the context of procedures and functions, as we shall see in Chapter 4.

Pronouns and anonymous values

The idea of the association between name and value is so emphasised in programming that we may lose sight of the fact that there are situations where it may be advantageous not to have a unique name for an object. This is the programming equivalent of the use of pronouns in natural language. Unfortunately we rarely turn to natural language for guiding precepts in programming language design.

The brain-washed programmer may see nothing unusual in the sequence

> **integer** n;
> *read* (n); *print*(n);

but the newcomer to the subject would find it much more obvious to write

> READ a number;
> PRINT it;

Pronouns are rare in programming languages, though NEBULA used QIH (quantity-in-hand). We find an example of completely anonymous values in POP-2. Processing in POP-2 involves an explicit stack: an isolated expression is evaluated and its value placed on the stack, and assignment is an operation that takes the top of the stack as an implicit operand. Thus the assignment

> $x + y \rightarrow z$;

can be written (eccentrically) as

> $x + y$;
> $\rightarrow z$;

A more useful application is instanced by the following example:

> $a, b \rightarrow a \rightarrow b$

which interchanges the values of a and b. Interchanging usually involves an explicitly-named temporary store: here the temporary storage is in the anonymity of the stack.

ALGOL 68 also includes anonymous values. The construction **loc real** (called a local generator) creates a reference to an undefined real value that is not linked to a name: pictorially

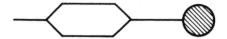

Such an object is a likely candidate as the value to be assigned to a **ref real** variable: the usefulness of this construction will be seen later.

3

EXPRESSIONS AND COMMANDS

"Stand by folks, we've done praying."
Comment attributed to a telegraph operator
on the occasion of the linking of the Union
Pacific and Central Pacific Railroads in 1869.

Expressions

The *expression* is a basic component of most languages. It is
made up of *operands*, which are variables or constants, and
operators (and also calls of functions, which we temporarily
ignore). The process of evaluation involves substituting values
for variable names, and carrying out the specified operations.
The following seemingly pedantic elaborations are important:

(1)   Strictly speaking, operators and variables are both
      represented by symbols. The evaluation process is to
      substitute values for all symbols, then the specified
      operations are carried out on the data values. (In
      most familiar languages the 'value' of an operation
      symbol is fixed, but there is no reason why this
      should necessarily be so.)

(2)   The 'value' of an operator may depend on its operands.
      Thus if i, j are integers and x, y are real, the '+' in
      $i + j$ has a meaning completely different from the '+'
      in $x + y$. An operator of this kind is called a
      polymorphic operator.

The values associated with the variables and operators form
the environment in which the evaluation takes place. It is a
seemingly obvious statement that the evaluation of an
expression should simply produce a value, with no change to
the environment, but this concept of *referential transparency*
is very important when we come to include functions. Since
an expression is just a complicated way of defining a value,
it ought to be possible to use an expression in place of a
variable in any context where a value is required. Unfortunately, this is not always so (e.g. FORTRAN DO-loops).

Commands

In contrast, a command is a program element that deliberately changes the environment: the most obvious example is an assignment. It is a matter of definition whether a command also has a value. One convention is that an assignment has as its value the value assigned, so that the command $a := b + 3.2$ has the value $b + 3.2$. This allows a consistent interpretation of a command like

$$a := b := c + d$$

which is implicitly bracketed

$$a := (b := c + d)$$

so that a is assigned the value of the assignment in brackets, i.e. $c + d$. The convention also allows interpretation of the less attractive possibility typified by the following statement:

$$a := b + (c := d*e) + f$$

which is equivalent to the pair of statements

$$c := d*e$$
$$a := b + c + f$$

An alternative convention is that the value of an assignment is the reference of the destination. We shall see shortly that this makes little or no difference in practice. Allowing commands to have values means that the distinction between conditional commands and conditional expressions largely disappears, and it is possible to have constructions like

if b **then** $u := x+y$; $v := x-y$; $u*v$ **else** 0

(In ALGOL 68 the terms command and expression do not occur; both are referred to as unitary clauses.)

Compound commands

A particularly useful feature of a language is the ability to group a set of commands into a compound command that can appear in any context where a single command is valid. Provision of such a feature in FORTRAN would make the logical-IF a much more useful construction.

ALGOL 60 uses **begin**...**end** to group commands into a compound command; ALGOL 68 allows the use of ordinary brackets as an alternative notation. In PL/I commands are grouped into a compound unit by DO...END : the result is called a "DO-group". Confusingly, DO is also used to

34

introduce repetition.

Compound commands find their greatest use in conditional and repetition constructions. Thus in ALGOL 60 we can write

if b **then begin** $x := y$; $y := z$ **end**

To obtain this effect in FORTRAN most programmers would write

```
    IF B THEN GOTO 10
    GOTO 11
10  X = Y
    Y = Z
11  .......
```

though it is better style to write

```
IF B THEN X = Y
IF B THEN Y = Z
```

Similarly, for repetition in ALGOL 60 we write

for ... do
   begin ... end

whereas in FORTRAN we require a label (statement number) to delimit the scope of the repetition controlled by DO. We observe in passing that the absence of compound commands in a language tends to give a proliferation of labels and goto's, and thus makes structured programming very difficult.

The evaluation of expressions

The apparently simple definition of an expression given earlier still leaves a remarkable amount of scope for the language designer to introduce variations. Least important is the cosmetic one of appearance:

    ADD A TO B GIVING C
and $C := A + B$

are, like the Colonel's Lady and Rosie O'Grady, sisters under the skin. Likewise, whether we indicate exponentiation by up-arrow or double asterisk is of little importance: the choice is determined largely by the character set available, and objections can only be made on aesthetic grounds.

Order of evaluation

More significant is whether the designer has assigned differing priorities to the various operators, thus imposing some order of evaluation. Most scientific languages follow the rule "multiplication and division before addition and subtraction", thus giving $a + b*c$ its familiar meaning, $a + (b*c)$. We should beware of familiar meanings, however – many a FORTRAN programmer has come to grief by assuming that A/2*B is the correct linearisation of $\frac{a}{2b}$.

Once we get beyond the simple arithmetic operators, problems arise because there is no longer an "obvious" relationship. (Quickly – how is X*Y**Z bracketed in FORTRAN? Is it the same in all versions of FORTRAN?) ALGOL 60 has seventeen different operators, and it has been aptly remarked that if you find a person who can tell you the relative precedence of $\equiv$ and $\supset$ you have found the man who wrote that part of the compiler. Given that no two languages assign the same priorities to the set of operators that they have in common, there is something to be said for the APL equal-priority rule. (Most critics of APL concentrate on the right-to-left evaluation rule, missing the fact that it is the equal-priority rule that is really significant.) However, in a language that keeps its data classes distinct (e.g. Booleans in a separate class from integers) a good deal of simplification can be achieved by using the fact that we know the class(es) of operand that each operator takes. Thus $a + b > c + d$ can be parsed without recourse to precedence rules, since the relational operator must take numeric arguments. We only need precedence relations within the group of operators that take operands from the same class. As so often in programming, the policy of "divide and rule" pays off.

Dereferencing

We have already noted that in the statement I = I+1 the I on the left stands for the reference, whereas the I on the right stands for the value. This automatic dereferencing of the I on the right is typical of most languages, though in BLISS, a system programming language, names always stand for references and an explicit operator has to be used to obtain a value. Thus in BLISS we would write I ← .I + 1, the dot being the dereferencing ("contents of") operator.

If references can themselves be values, then the rules for automatic dereferencing have to be carefully thought out. The ALGOL 68 rules are as follows

    (i)   No automatic dereferencing is ever applied on the left of an assignment.

    (ii) The mode of the reference delivered by the left-hand

side determines the kind of value to be yielded by the right-hand side. If possible, the rhs will be "coerced" to yield the right kind of value by automatic dereferencing.

(iii) Both arguments of a comparison are dereferenced.

Some examples will assist in understanding this. Suppose we have declarations

real x, y, z ;
ref real xx;

then the mode of x is **ref real**, and the mode of xx is **ref ref real**. If we have the assignment

$x := 3.4$;

this can be done immediately: x is a reference to a real, 3.4 is a real value, so the assignment is compatible.

Similarly, if we have

$xx := x$;

then the value of xx becomes the reference x. It is now legitimate to write

$y := xx$;

y is a **ref real** so requires a **real** value, consequently xx will be dereferenced twice.

Although dereferencing never occurs automatically on the left of an assignment, it can be forced by explicit use of the prefix **val**. Thus

val $xx : = 4.0$

is a legitimate way of setting x to the value 4.0.

Mixed-mode expressions

We have already noted that operators like +, – etc. are polymorphic, having differing meanings depending on the attributes of their operands. Particular attention must be given to the questions that arise if the attributes of the two operands are not identical. FORTRAN tries to avoid the problem by forbidding such mixed-mode expressions as far as possible: PL/I goes to the other extreme by allowing any conceivable combination of variables.

There are two ways of dealing with mixed-mode expressions. The first method is to provide a table for each operator in which the rows and columns are labelled by the types of operand and the table entries give the type of result (and by implication the transformation to be applied to the operands). For example

operator +, −

	real	double length	integer
real	real	double[1]	real[2]
double length	double[1]	double	double[3]
integer	real[2]	double[3]	integer

Actions:

(1) Extend single-length argument
(2) Float integer argument
(3) Float and extend integer argument

The second approach is to have a "target" type for each operator in an expression, and a table to determine the transformations to be carried out to achieve the correct target type. In most cases it will make little difference which method is used. Thus if we have X = X + I + J with X real, I, J integer, method (1) will evaluate the right-hand side as X + FLOAT(I+J), whilst the second method will evaluate X + FLOAT(I)+ FLOAT(J). The final result will be the same, unless I + J gives integer overflow. However if division is involved we have a different story. FORTRAN will evaluate

$$X = X + I/J$$
as $$X = X + FLOAT(I/J)$$

whereas the programmer probably intended X = X + FLOAT(I) /FLOAT(J) which is unlikely to give the same result. (Remember that integer divide in FORTRAN gives quotient without remainder.)

The difference between the two approaches can be illustrated using the tree representation of the statement thus:

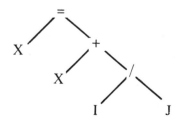

The first method works "bottom-up", thus it finds I/J, an

integer division with an integer result, a "real-integer" addition which causes the integer value to be floated before the real addition takes place.

In contrast the second method works "top-down" as follows:

(i) destination is a real variable, so a real value is required
(ii) hence the '+' is real plus
(iii) hence the '/' is real divide, and the table will say that real divide needs real operands
(iv) hence I and J will be floated

Languages usually include explicit (built-in) functions by which the programmer can force particular representation conversions (e.g. FLOAT and IFIX in FORTRAN). ALGOL 68 provides a syntactic device (called a cast): if for example an expression is prefixed by **real val** this will ensure that the expression is evaluated to yield a **real** result, if this is possible. (This is the same mechanism that is used to achieve explicit dereferencing.) A transformation from integer to real, or from real to complex, is called a "widening", since it can be achieved without any loss of information. Automatic invocation of transformations that may throw away information (as for example in the FORTRAN assignment $I = X$) are to be deprecated (and are explicitly forbidden in ALGOL 68).

As more representations are introduced in a language, the problems of mixed modes increase. For example, if numbers can be stored in binary or as binary-coded-decimal character strings, can these two be mixed? An example of such mixing would be the COBOL expression

IF QUANTITY IS EQUAL TO "123"
or   MOVE "34" TO QUANTITY

where QUANTITY has the attribute COMPUTATIONAL and quotes denote literal character constants.

In PL/I a further level of complication is introduced by the fact that declarations (particularly of fixed-point quantities) can include a specification of precision, so that account has to be taken of the situation where the two operands of an arithmetic operation differ in precision, though having other-wise identical attributes. PL/I has elaborate rules which some-times lead to unexpected consequences. For example, if default attributes are used the expression $(1/3+25)$ will yield the value 5.33333333333333. This is because the rules for division give a precision of (15,14) for the evaluation of 1/3 (i.e. 15 digits, 14 after the decimal point). The rules for addition require that the result have the precision of the highest precision operand, so the final result can only have one place before the decimal point, causing the true result 25.33333...3 to be truncated. Such behaviour might reasonably be regarded as deplorable: equally deplorable is the fact that the correct result is obtained if the expression is written (01/3 + 25), since the precision of 01/3 is (15, 13). Such significance of a "non-significant" zero is against all expectation. In fairness it should be pointed out that it is possible for the PL/I programmer to be warned of this situation. Truncation of a leftmost digit is an instance of a SIZE error, and the programmer can specify that standard error action is to be taken, or his own error routine entered, when such an error occurs. However, incredible as it may seem, the default situation if the programmer does not specify otherwise is to ignore SIZE errors.

The situation gets even more complicated if both representation conversion and precision matching occur in the same statement. For example, suppose we have two PL/I variables Q and N with attributes

> Q : fixed decimal (10, 5)
>   i.e. 10 digits, 5 after decimal point
> N : fixed binary, 15 bits

and we obey the program

$$N = 0 \; ;$$
$$Q = N + .1;$$

The PL/I rules cause the .1 to be converted to binary with precision 5,4 thus the recurring binary fraction corresponding to 0.1_{10} (0.000110001100011....) is truncated to 0.0001. Binary addition is then performed and the result is converted back to decimal with precision 10,5 yielding 0.06250 as the final value for Q. This is, to say the least, surprising. However, PL/I provides built-in functions to force particular representations (compare ALGOL 68 casts), so that the correct result could be obtained by writing Q = DEC(N) + .1 , thus ensuring decimal addition. This is one example of a more general facility for controlling the precision of a computation. A situation where this is useful is the calculation of a double-precision inner product from two single-precision vectors, in order to avoid contamination of the product by round-off and truncation. (Such a requirement frequently arises in linear algebra.) Suppose that X,Y are single precision vectors with attributes FLOAT DECIMAL(6), and Z is a double precision variable with attributes FLOAT DECIMAL(16). If the inner loop contained the statement

$$Z = Z + X(I)*Y(I)$$

the product would be formed single precision, then widened to double precision by extending with zeros (a fruitless exercise). If however we were to write

$$Z = Z + X(I)*PREC(Y(I),16)$$

the precision of Y would be changed to double precision by appending zeros; the context rules would then cause X to be similarly extended and the multiplication and subsequent addition would be carried out double-length. The same effect can be obtained by writing

$$Z = Z + MULTIPLY(X(I),Y(I),16)$$

This form is to be preferred on grounds of style.

More about commands

At the beginning of this chapter we introduced the concept of the command as something that changes the environment in which evaluation takes place. Commands can be subdivided into two classes:

assignment – these commands change the environment explicitly by giving new values to variables

control and
sequencing – these commands change the environment implicitly by selecting the next command to be obeyed, and possibly changing the values of "hidden" counters.

Assignment commands

In the light of the discussion in Chapter 2 we can say that the general form of the assignment is

$$\epsilon 1 := \epsilon 2$$

where $\epsilon 1$ is an expression that yields a reference and $\epsilon 2$ is an expression that yields an appropriate value. Languages vary in the restrictions placed on the form of the expressions $\epsilon 1$, $\epsilon 2$: typically $\epsilon 1$ must be a trivially simple expression (a variable name or an indexed array name). Many languages allow multiple assignment, as for example ALGOL 68:

$$x := y := 4.3;$$

Here the assignment to y is done first: the value of the unitary clause $y := 4.3$ is its left-hand side (the reference associated with y) and this is dereferenced to give 4.3 as the value to be assigned to x.

Two non-obvious aspects of multiple assignments in other languages should be noted.

(i) COBOL allows multiple assignments of the form

ADD A TO B, C, D

meaning $B \leftarrow A + B$
$C \leftarrow A + C$
$D \leftarrow A + D$

It also permits

ADD A TO B, C(B), D

which does not do what the programmer probably intended.

(ii) In PL/I the form of the multiple assignment is

$A, B = C$

The hapless programmer who writes

$A = B = C$

is in for a big surprise. The statement is recognised as the assignment $A = (B = C)$ and the condition $B = C$ is evaluated, yielding the one-bit string '0' or '1'. The type conversion mechanism will then browbeat this into a form compatible with A, and the net result will be to set A to zero or one in the appropriate base, mode and precision. We observe in passing the folly of using the same sign to denote both equality and assignment, and the danger of over-enthusiastic type-conversion.

Not to be confused with multiple assignment is the simultaneous or collateral assignment, e.g.

$a, b, c := x, y, z$

This usually appears in a context where the left-hand side specifies part of an array or structure.

Control and sequencing

Commands are normally executed in sequence. This may be indicated by writing them on separate lines, or they may be delimited by a particular character, commonly a semi-colon. Although this delimiter may only be a syntactic device, it is useful to regard it as an operator that causes the preceding command to be obeyed. This leaves it open to introduce

42

another delimiter that does not imply such rigid sequencing
e.g.

> S1; S2; S3; S4;
> indicates a sequence of four statements (commands),
> whereas
> S1, S2; S3, S4;
> implies that S1, S2 are to be obeyed before S3, S4
> but that the sequencing between S1, S2 is immaterial,
> as is that between S3, S4.

Breaks in the normal sequence are effected by special commands or command structures. Traditionally, the most common form of sequencing is the **goto** and label. Modern thinking places much more emphasis on commands that select alternatives and control looping: these make it much easier to write structured programs. We shall follow this trend and defer consideration of **goto** to the end of this chapter.

Selection commands

There are three basic selection commands:

> (a) conditional execution: **if** b **then** S

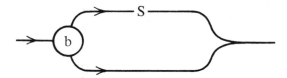

> (b) two alternative selection:
> **if** b **then** $S1$ **else** $S2$

> (c) multiple
> choice
> selection

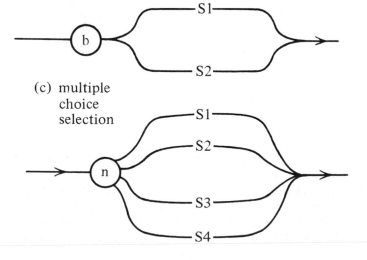

We first observe that (a) is a special case of (b), i.e.

>**if** *b* **then** *S*1 **else** *donothing*;

and that whilst the control variable in (b) is a **Boolean**, in (c) it must be an integer.

FORTRAN provides only a restricted form of conditional command: since there are no compound commands the logical-IF is of little utility except as a conditional jump. ALGOL 60 provides both types (a) and (b), that is

>**if** *b* **then** *S*
>
>and **if** *b* **then** *S*1 **else** *S*2

S, *S*1, and *S*2 can be compound statements: *S*2 can be another conditional statement, but it is not permitted to write an **if** after a **then**. This restriction is necessary in order to resolve the ambiguity of the "dangling else". If the restriction were not imposed it would be possible to write

>**if** *b*1 **then if** *b*2 **then** *S*1 **else** *S*2

which could be parsed as

>**if** *b*1 **then** [**if** *b*2 **then** *S*1 **else** *S*2]
>
>or   **if** *b*   **then** [**if** *b*2 **then** *S*1] **else** *S*2

If it is really required to have an **if** after a **then** it can be done in ALGOL 60, e.g.

>**if** *b*1 **then**
>>**begin if** *b*2 **then** *S*1 **end**
>>**else** *S*2;

Such constructions tend to be difficult to comprehend: on stylistic grounds one would prefer to write the above as

>**if** *b*1 ∧ *b*2 **then** *S*1;
>
>**if** ⌐*b*1 **then** *S*2;

On the other hand, an **if** after an **else** is a useful and perspicuous structure, e.g.

if *b*1 **then** *S*1 **else if** *b*2 **then** *S*2 **else if** *b*3 **then** *S*3 **else** *S*4;

tests conditions *b*1, *b*2, *b*3 in turn and selects the paired statement, selecting *S*4 if none of the conditions is satisfied.

POP-2 and ALGOL 68 get round the dangling else problem by requiring each **if** to be paired with a "closing bracket", **close** in POP-2 and **fi** in ALGOL 68. Thus the potential ambiguity in ALGOL 60 is clearly resolved: we write either

> if $b1$ then if $b2$ then $S1$ close
>> else $S2$ close

or

> if $b1$ then
>> if $b2$ then $S1$ else $S2$ close
>
> close

An incidental advantage of explicitly matching the **if** with a "closing bracket" is that it removes the need to group a sequence of statements between **then** and **else** into a compound statement by the use of **begin** and **end**. A disadvantage of this scheme is that the testing of a number of conditions in succession becomes clumsy e.g. in ALGOL 68

> if $b1$ then $S1$
>> else if $b2$ then $S2$
>>> else if $b3$ then $S3$
>>>> else $S4$ fi fi fi

Apart from the extra writing, the construction is error-prone (it is easy to think that 4 **fi**'s are needed in the above example). ALGOL 68 allows **else if** and the matching **fi** to be elided to **elif**: POP-2 uses **elseif** for the same purpose, giving an eminently readable construction

> if $b1$ then $S1$
>> elseif $b2$ then $S2$
>>> elseif $b3$ then $S3$
>>>> else $S4$ close;

PL/I provides both kinds of conditional:

> IF b THEN S;
> IF b THEN $S1$; ELSE $S2$;

(Note the irritating semi-colon before the ELSE.) The statements can be compound (DO groups).

PL/I solves the problem of the "dangling else" by requiring a dummy ELSE clause to resolve ambiguity. The rule about if-after-then (PL/I calls this a "nested if") is that if any **if** requires an **else**, then all deeper nested **if**s must have corresponding **else** clauses, which may be null. Thus

> IF $b1$ THEN IF $b2$ THEN $S1$; ELSE $S2$;

is parsed as

> IF $b1$ THEN [IF $B2$ THEN $S1$; ELSE $S2$]

and the alternative meaning is obtained by adding a dummy ELSE:

45

IF $b1$ THEN IF $b2$ THEN $S1$; ELSE; ELSE $S2$;

Conditionals in COBOL follow a similar pattern. The basic structure is

IF *condition* THEN *statement*-1 ELSE *statement*-2.

The special case NEXT STATEMENT is allowed as an alternative after the THEN or the ELSE, and the sequence "ELSE NEXT STATEMENT" can be elided, giving a simple IF... THEN structure. COBOL displays one original feature. As in all languages, the predicate following the IF can be a compound predicate, made up by combining simple predicates with the connectives "and" and "or" (i.e. a Boolean expression). If we wish to establish set membership, in most languages we have an unfortunately repetitious expression e.g.

if (*year* = 1960) $\vee$ (*year* = 1972) $\vee$ (*year* = 1984) **then**...

In COBOL this can be abbreviated by "factoring out" the common subject of the predicate, thus:

IF YEAR IS EQUAL TO 1960 OR 1972 OR 1984 THEN...

This construction can be misleading, since the condition (year $\neq$ 1970) **and** (year $\neq$ 1974) is written YEAR IS NOT EQUAL TO 1970 OR 1974. Although the designers of COBOL probably did not realise it, they were attempting to incorporate the concept of set membership. Using the mathematical set membership operator ϵ in its usual sense, the condition is

if *year* ϵ $\{1960, 1972, 1984\}$

APL and PASCAL provide such an operation.

COBOL allows nested IF's, e.g.

```
IF P
  IF Q
    PERFORM A
  ELSE
    PERFORM B
  PERFORM C
ELSE
  PERFORM D
```

This is a misleading construction: in the above example C is not obeyed when Q is true.

It is strange that writers on COBOL and PL/I should emphasise the use of nested IF's of the form **if...then if...** since this is inherently difficult for the human mind to comprehend. Humans are not good at stacking information, and easily lose track of the pending **else**'s. By contrast, **if**..

then .. elseif .. is a "natural" construction to the human reader.

We may note in passing that where the predicate is a compound one, considerable economies in time may be obtained if the evaluation is stopped as soon as the value of the expression is determined. (Since $x \wedge$ **false** = **false**, and $x \vee$ **true** = **true**, whatever the value of x, the value of a Boolean expression may often be determined quite early in the evaluation of the expression.) If side-effects are forbidden, then no harm can come from not completing the evaluation. If the programmer makes use of side effects, this strategy might lead to a particularly nasty and difficult-to-discover error in the results: this is another argument for viewing side-effects with the greatest suspicion. POP-2 offers two forms of conditional: one where evaluation stops as soon as possible and one where complete evaluation is guaranteed. Thus

> **if** $a = 0$ **or** $1/a = b$ **then** ...
> and **if** $boolor$ ($(a = 0)$, $(1/a = b)$) **then** ...

are equivalent except that if a is zero the second form will cause arithmetic overflow since both arguments of the Boolean "or" will be evaluated. Here the function boolor is the usual "or" function of Boolean algebra, whereas the **or** is a shorthand: p **or** q = **if** p **then** *true* **elseif** q **then** *true* **else** *false* **close**. Similarly, p **and** q = **if** p **then** q **else** *false* **close**. McCarthy introduced this construction in LISP under the name "sequential conjunction".

The predicate after an IF is commonly a relation. However, most languages allow Boolean variables, and these can be used as the predicate, which can lead to an increase in the readability of programs e.g.

> **integer** *balance* ; **boolean** *overdrawn*;
> ......
> *overdrawn* := *balance* < 0 ;
> ......
> **if** *overdrawn* **then** ....

PL/I does not have Boolean variables: formally the predicate after **if** must evaluate to a bit-string: if any bit in the string is set to 1 this indicates **true**, whilst **false** is represented by either a string of all zeros or a null string. In the case of a 1-bit string this amounts to the same thing as a Boolean variable, but the generality of the definition does leave the way open for low cunning and dirty tricks.

COBOL, as we might expect, has a rather unusual form of

Boolean variable. We can associate with a variable a number of "condition names" and with each condition name we associate a list of literal values which, if taken by the main variable, will cause the condition-name to take the value **true**. For example, in a file definition we could write

> 02   YEAR-IN-RESIDENCE
>   88   FRESHMAN VALUE IS 1
>   88   SOPHOMORE VALUES ARE 2 THRU 3
>   88   SENIOR VALUE 4

(Note the use of level 88 to identify condition names.) We can now write

> IF SOPHOMORE THEN ....

and SOPHOMORE will have the value TRUE if YEAR-IN-RESIDENCE has the value 2 or 3.

Multiple selection commands

We now turn to the multiple selection command, which is a generalisation of the FORTRAN computed GOTO in the same way that **if .. then** is a generalisation of the conditional jump. This construction has only recently appeared in languages in the form of the **case** statement. In ALGOL 68 it takes the form

>   **case** n **in** $S1, S2, S3 \ldots S_j$ **esac**
> or   **case** n **in** $S1, S2 \ldots S_j$ **out** S_k **esac**

n is an integer (or a clause yielding an integer value), and the S's are serial clauses (compound or simple statements/expressions). If $n = 1$ the first S is selected, if $n = 2$ the second S is selected and so on. The second form provides a default exit S_k to be taken if the value of n exceeds j.

The only disadvantage of this construction is that it is not particularly readable since it is necessary to count the S's to find the one that will be obeyed in a particular situation. For this reason an alternative form of case statement has been proposed in PASCAL in which each alternative group is labelled, e.g.

>   **case** V **of**
> $L1$: $S1$;
> $L2$: $S2$;
> $L3$: $S3$;
>
>   ⋮
>
> Ln: Sn
>   **end**

Here V is a variable whose value will be one of the labels $L1$, $L2$, etc.

Repetition statements

There are only two basic variants of the repetition statement,

    (i)   repetition controlled by a computed condition

and (ii)   repetition controlled by an explicit count or list of values.

The first form has two alternatives

      while b **do** S

  and S **repeat while** b

Here b is a condition and S a (compound) statement. The difference between the two forms is that in the second case the statement S is always obeyed at least once, whereas in the first case it may not be obeyed at all. It is a trivial bit of syntactic decoration to replace **while** by **until**. The use of **repeat ... while** is a powerful tool in achieving "go-to-less" programming.

    The other sort of loop is of the form

      for *variable* := < *list of elements* >
      do *compound statement*;

Here < list of elements > can be an explicit list or can be a generator of the form n **to** m **by** k. In such loops there is often a possibility of premature termination because an exception condition has arisen. Classically this is dealt with by a **goto** transferring control out of the loop, but from the point of view of structured programming this is undesirable, and a common solution is to include a "while clause" in the loop specification, thus

      for *variable* := < *list of elements* > **while** < *condition*>
      do <*compound statement*> ;

If we make <*condition*> the logical complement of the exception condition this ensures that the loop can be prematurely terminated. We still require a test at the end of the loop to find out if we dropped out or if we were pushed, e.g.

      for i := n **to** m **by** k **while** $a > 0$
      do begin ...
          ...
          ...
      end;
      if $a > 0$ **then** *normal exit* **else** *exception*;

We may note that the above notation combines the two kinds of looping, since by making the $<$ *list of elements* $>$ trivial we can make the "while" control the loop.

We now look briefly at the way looping is achieved in various languages.

FORTRAN has the most restrictive form – the simple DO loop that allows for an integer control variable incremented by integer amounts in a positive direction.

ALGOL 60 provides a variety of mechanisms based on the **for** loop.

for ... step ... until

gives the equivalent of the FORTRAN DO loop without the restriction to integer control variable and positive steps. Alternatively an explicit list of values can be provided, e.g.

for $x: = 1.3, 1.75, 25.0, 33.1$

or a **while** clause can be added, e.g.

for $j : = 3, j+1$ **while** $f(j) > 0$

PL/I facilities parallel closely those of ALGOL 60 with syntactic differences. Loops are introduced by DO, and the control variable is specified in the form FROM/TO/BY, with the option of changing the order, e.g. FROM/BY/TO or omitting one or more components (in which case defaults are used). A WHILE option is also available. ALGOL 68 provides almost identical facilities.

COBOL provides a variety of looping forms in a typically verbose way. The verb PERFORM is used (this also introduces procedure calls) and typical variants are

(i) PERFORM ——— n TIMES
(ii) PERFORM ——— VARYING —— FROM ——
     BY —— UNTIL

The first is self evident. The second form should not be confused with the apparently similar ALGOL 60 form since the COBOL UNTIL specifies a terminating *condition*, not the final value to be taken by the control variable. It is thus strictly analogous to the **while** clause of ALGOL or PL/I.

A particular point of language design in the context of loops is the status of the control variable. Is it "hidden" or can it be changed within the body of the loop? For example, if we write in FORTRAN

```
        DO 10 I = 1, 10
        ....
        I = I + 2
        ....
10      CONTINUE
```

will I increase in steps of 1 or 3? (The Standard says 1: many compilers would make it increase in steps of 3.)

Control transfers

The **goto** is one of the most intuitively obvious, and at the same time most dangerous, constructions in programming languages. On an abstract level **goto** is undesirable because it destroys structuring within a program. On a practical level immense complications arise as soon as we depart from the simplest situations.

The simple FORTRAN GOTO does not present difficulty: it refers to a numerical statement label that is attached to another statement in the same subroutine or function segment. In ALGOL 60 the label becomes an alphanumeric identifier, and the **goto** has to be restricted to prevent jumping into the middle of a block (consequently avoiding the declarations at the block head). Thus the scope of a label is restricted to the smallest surrounding block.

FORTRAN with its computed GOTO, and ALGOL 60 with its switch, allow a multiway branch in a fairly straightforward manner, but if we try to go any further complication sets in. As an example we may take the FORTRAN assigned GOTO. The ASSIGN statement allows an integer variable to take a statement number as its value, and this can later be used as the destination of a GOTO. However, the restrictions that no arithmetic can be performed on the statement number, and that the GOTO must list all possible destinations, make the construction useless in practice.

COBOL allows dynamic changing of control transfers by the ALTER verb. Thus if we have

        P1. GOTO S1.

we can somewhere else write

        ALTER P1 TO PROCEED TO S2.

which when obeyed will change the destination of the GOTO. This means that the program as obeyed may differ materially from the program as written, a sure recipe for disaster.

51

PL/I allows "label variables", i.e. a variable can be declared with "label" as an attribute, and can then be used in a **goto** to give a truly dynamic jump. Explicit labels in the program e.g.

L1: A = B

are treated as implicit initialised declarations of label variables. Although superficially attractive the problems of scope and jumping in and out of blocks make this a very dangerous facility.

The only remotely satisfactory form of dynamic label is in APL: since every line of an APL function is numbered, the **goto** (written as a right arrow) can have as its argument any integer expression that evaluates to a valid line number. An invalid line number in a **goto** is used to signal exit from a function, so that an error in program logic may have unexpected and undetected effects.

4

FUNCTIONS AND PROCEDURES

Enter a Company of mutinous Citizens, with
staves, clubs, and other weapons.
Stage Directions, Act I,
Coriolanus.

Basic Notions

Most languages provide a facility for breaking a program up
into a number of self-contained modules that communicate
with each other in a precisely-defined and fairly rigid way.
It is this policy of "divide-and-rule" that makes the
programming of large projects feasible. Thus we encounter
the need to deal with more complicated structures than simple
commands and expressions. The first stage of elaboration is to
attach a name to an expression (the STATEMENT FUNCTION
of FORTRAN). Thus we might write (in FORTRAN)

$$F(X) = A*X**2 + B*X + C$$

We note that X is a *dummy variable*: the meaning is not
changed if we replace X by Y throughout, since when this
function is used as a component in an expression, the right-
hand side will be evaluated using the argument supplied in
place of X. Some terminology can be introduced here. F is the
function name, X is a *formal parameter*, and the expression on
the right of the equals is the *function body*. The argument
supplied when the function is used is called an *actual parameter*.
Simply attaching a name to an expression in this way is
restrictive: we often require to define a function whose value
is obtained as a result of obeying a sequence of commands.
FORTRAN and ALGOL 60 both provide this facility in the
form of "function sub-programs" and "type procedures"
respectively. Another useful device is to attach a name to a
sequence of commands: we call the resultant object a *routine*
(cf. FORTRAN subroutine, ALGOL procedure). Again, it is
convenient to have formal parameters that are replaced by
actual parameters when the routine is called.

In FORTRAN the subprograms (routines and functions) are
more-or-less independent entities. In ALGOL 60, procedures
and type-procedures are defined at block-heads, and therefore

have a scope like any variable. PL/I calls such procedures "internal procedures", but also allows "external procedures" which have a global scope. (The static nesting of procedures in ALGOL 60 and PL/I should not be confused with the dynamic nesting that occurs at execution time when one procedure calls another.)

Notation for functions

In ALGOL 60 and FORTRAN the value of a function is determined by an assignment to a variable having the same name as the function. For example:

FORTRAN	ALGOL 60
FUNCTION G(X, Y)	**real procedure** $g(x,y)$;
U = X + Y	**real** x,y;
V = X - Y	**begin real** u,v;
G = U*V	$u := x + y$; $v := x - y$;
RETURN	$g := u*v$
END	**end**

This is a sloppy notation, since it does not distinguish between the function itself and the value obtained by applying the function to an argument. (This is an important distinction to make if one wants to manipulate functions as data objects.) If g is a function, then in any assignment to g the value assigned should be another function body, i.e. a piece of program. PL/I gets round this difficulty by writing the value of the function after the RETURN statement thus:

```
....
U = X + Y
V = X - Y
RETURN (U*V)
END
```

Another possibility is to use a special notation, e.g.

$u := x + y$; $v := x - y$;
result is $u*v$
end

Alternatively, it is possible to adopt the convention that the value associated with a sequence of commands and/or expressions is the last value computed: the function body in the above example would then be just

$u := x + y$; $v := x - y$; $u*v$ **end**

This convention applies particularly well in a stack-based

system. If the value of an expression is placed on the stack when computed (as in POP-2), then the last expression will give the value on the top of the stack at function exit, which is almost a definition of a function value. The convention also allows a consistent way of defining functions with more than one result. (A simple example of such a function is division with remainder. A more complicated example is a quadrature procedure whose values are the value of the integral and a bound on its error.) POP-2 defines the value of a function as those values (except for local variables) that are on the stack at the end of the function but were not on the stack at the start. Thus the function body

$$u := x + y; \ v := x - y;$$
$$u * v, \ u/v;$$

would leave two values on the stack as its "value".

Whatever the mechanism used to return the result, we should also consider what the result can be. FORTRAN, ALGOL and PL/I restrict the result to being a simple scalar object (real, integer, Boolean or possibly complex): note particularly that arrays cannot be returned as function values. More advanced languages such as ALGOL 68 and POP-2 allow functions whose values are arrays, structures, function bodies or references. The difficulties that arise when the value of a function is a reference are discussed later.

Side effects

Allowing a function to be computed as the result of several commands immediately opens up the possibility of side effects. For example, consider the following situation in FORTRAN.

```
      SUBROUTINE H(X)
      COMMON A
      . . . .
      A = A + 1
      . . . .
      H = . . . .
      RETURN
      END
```

Suppose the main program includes the following:

```
      COMMON A
      . . . .
      A = 1.0
      X = 2.3
      Y = A + H(X)
```

Evaluating the expression A + H(X) now has the effect of changing the environment, and the value yielded will depend on the order in which the expression is evaluated.

If the concept of referential transparency is to be maintained then a function must not change the environment, i.e. side-effects must be forbidden. A routine necessarily changes the environment, but we may still require that the changes be a result of explicit action rather than hidden side-effects. We are thus led to consider the ways in which a function or routine communicates with its surroundings. This can be in one of two ways, either via the parameters passed to the function/routine when it is called, or by reference to objects defined outside the body of the function/routine (the *non-local* variables). We consider parameter-passing first.

Parameter passing

When a routine or function is called the actual parameters provided in the call have to be substituted for the formal parameters in the function body. There are various methods of effecting this substitution, and they may be broadly classified into three groups

   (i)   pass values
   (ii) pass references
   (iii) defer processing of actual parameters until
         they are actually used.

In the first two methods the *calling* program decides what kind of parameter to pass to the function/routine. If an unevaluated parameter is passed, then the *called* function/routine can decide whether to treat the parameters as values or references. We immediately observe that the way to control side effects is to pass values. It is impossible to change the environment without a reference.

The method of passing values is sometimes called "call by value". It is appropriate for parameters of functions (except "left-hand functions", see below) since it gives full protection against side-effects. (If an attempt is made to assign a value to a formal parameter in a function body, this will be faulted at run-time since it will not be possible to obtain the required reference.) An incidental advantage is that the actual parameter is only evaluated once, with a consequent gain in efficiency if it is an expression, or involves subscripting an array. If we have a function of the form

        function $f(x,y)$; **real** x,y ;
        $< function\ body >$

and we transmit values, then when the function is called it is
as if declarations are inserted as follows:

> **function** $f(x,y)$;
> **real** x = *actual value*;
> **real** y = *actual value*;

Note that these are constant definitions. Pictorially the effect
is as follows.

Main program   **Function**

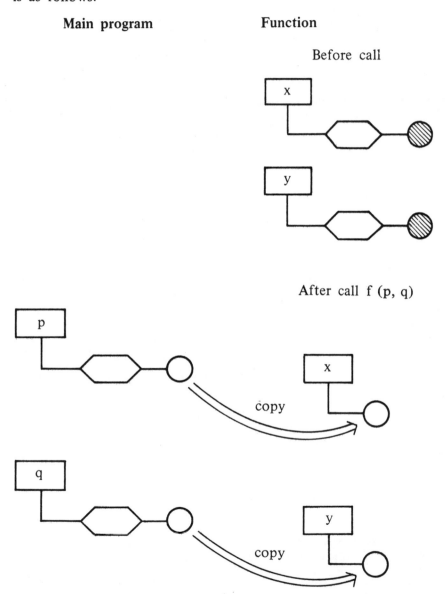

Before call

After call f (p, q)

copy

copy

In some systems (e.g. ALGOL 60) there is a subtle difference:

the effective declarations are

> **function** $f(x,y)$;
> **real** x := *actual value*;
> **real** y := *actual value*;

Here we have initialised (but not constant) declarations: after the call $f(p,q)$ the situation is

Main program   **Function**

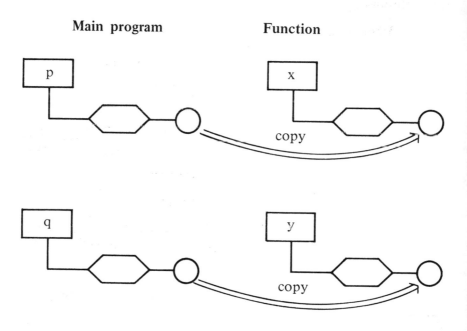

The difference is that in the first case it is impossible to assign to x or y; in the second case it is possible to make assignments, but these will affect *copies* of the actual parameters at run-time, and these copies will be thrown away when evaluation of the function is completed.

The method of passing references is sometimes called "call by reference", (or "call by simple name") and is the method used in FORTRAN. It is a general method which allows assignments to formal parameters. If we have the definition

> **function** $f(x,y)$; **real** x,y;
> < *function body* >

and references are transmitted, then it is as if declarations are inserted as follows when $f(p,q)$ is called:

> **real** $x \simeq p$;
> **real** $y \simeq q$;
> < *function body* >

Pictorially

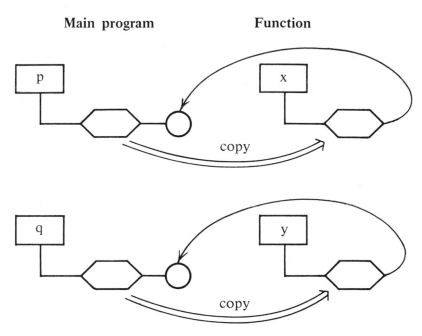

Main program   **Function**

Passing references leads to a number of complications. For example, suppose in FORTRAN we have

    FUNCTION G(X, Y)

    .
    .
    .
    .
    .

    X = 3.2

    .
    .
    .
    .

    END

and in the main program we include a call such as G(7.4,Q). For the first parameter there will be passed over a reference to a storage cell holding the constant 7.4. The effect of the assignment to X in the subroutine will be to change the contents of the storage cell containing 7.4. Now a practical compiler will probably arrange to hold only one copy of a constant: each time the constant is used another reference to the same storage cell is generated. If this has happened, the call G(7.4,Q) will have had the remarkable side-effect of changing the value of the constant 7.4 for all subsequent instructions. This would lead to wrong results, and would be a very difficult fault to diagnose. If the constant involved had been a frequently occurring one (such as 1) the effect on the program would be dramatic.

Another difficulty with passing references arises when the actual parameter is an expression. In this circumstance it is necessary to evaluate the expression, place it in a storage cell and pass a reference to the newly created storage cell as the actual parameter. It will still be possible to change the contents of this cell by an assignment in the function body, but such an assignment is likely to be confusing since in the main program there is no reference to this storage cell associated with a name. Thus any value assigned in the subroutine/function will be lost on return to the main program.

Variants of these schemes are used in order to get over the difficulties. In PL/I, for example, a parameter that is a variable name (or a single array element) is called by reference, whereas a parameter that is an expression (or a constant) is called by value. This is a reasonable compromise, except that the rules define anything in brackets as an expression, so that

CALL FRED (A)

does not necessarily have the same effect as

CALL FRED ((A))

(In the second case A is called by value.) This is confusing since a pair of apparently redundant brackets has a possibly important significance. There are also inconsistencies between the treatment of programmer defined functions and built in functions. Elementary programming courses often give a rule-of-thumb to guide the choice of the way in which parameters are passed, which is that call-by-value should be used unless it is intended to assign a value to the formal parameter in the body of the function. This avoids the diseconomy of repeatedly evaluating array subscripts, for example. However, it should be noted that if the parameter is an array, call-by-value will cause a copy of the array to be made, and call-by-reference or name is much more economical in space in this case.

Deferred processing of parameters

This technique, introduced into ALGOL 60 as "call by name", is the most powerful form of parameter passing: it is also the most dangerous and probably the most inefficient in general.

Though apparently straightforward, it is a subtle and difficult concept to appreciate fully. Instead of passing over a value or a reference we pass a rule by which the parameter may be evaluated. A formal definition is that the effect is as if all occurrences of the formal parameter in the function (routine) body had been textually replaced by the character string provided as the actual parameter in the call, with the proviso that the actual parameters are evaluated in the context of the call, not the context in which they appear in the function body after substitution.

If the parameter is a simple scalar variable, call-by-name is exactly the same as call-by-reference. If it is an expression made up of scalar variables the effect is the same as call-by-value, except that the expression is evaluated every time the parameter is referred to rather than once only on entry. If the parameter consists of or contains an array element then the difference is that with call-by-name the subscripts are evaluated every time the parameter is referred to, whereas with call by value or call by reference the values of the subscripts on entry are "frozen". This may or may not make a difference in practice. The simple rule given above for the interpretation of call by name leads to some difficulties.

For example, suppose we have

> **function** $f(x) = a*x + 3$;
> $a := f(b + c)$

Literal substitution of the parameter would make the function body

> $a* b + c + 3$

which is not the desired result. To get round this the actual parameter, if an expression, must be enclosed in brackets.

Another difficulty is illustrated in the next example.

> **function** $f(x,y)$; **real** x,y;
> **begin real** s,t;
> $s := x + y$;
> $t := x - y$;
>   **result is** $s*t$
> **end**;
> $a := f(t,n)$

Substitution of t for x in the body will lead to a clash of names, t being used for two different purposes. The compiler must make systematic name changes to avoid the clash. (This is possible since by its very nature a formal parameter can be systematically re-named without changing the meaning of the function/routine body.)

Call-by-name can lead the programmer astray, giving unexpected results. For example, consider

```
routine exchange (a,b); real a,b;
begin real t;
t := a; a := b; b := t
end
```

If this routine is called thus:

```
exchange (i,A[i]);
```

then literal substitution of the actual parameters produces the body

$$t := i; \quad i := A[i]; \quad A[i] := t$$

which is not the desired effect. (Note the call-by-reference would give the expected effect.)

Call-by-name is exploited by a trick known as Jensen's device. This depends on the fact that an array element can be legitimately specified as the actual parameter corresponding to a scalar formal parameter, and then exploiting the fact that since call-by-name passes the rule for accessing the array element, this can be used to access all the elements of the array.

Jensen's device is illustrated by the following (classic) example in ALGOL 60

```
begin
real array A [1:10], B[1:20, 1:30]; real x,y; integer i,j;
real procedure sigma (a,i,n); value n;
real a; integer n; integer i;
    begin real s; s := 0;
        for i := 1 step 1 until n do
        s := s + a;
    sigma := s
    end;
< code to assign values to A and B >
x := sigma (A[i],i,10);
y := sigma (sigma(B[i,j],i,20),j,30)
end
```

The effect of the assignments is to set $x = \sum_i A_i$ and

$y = \sum_i \sum_j B_{ij}$. Consider first the assignment to x. When sigma is called its argument n has the value 10, so by the rules for call-by-name the loop becomes

62

for i := 1 **step** 1 **until** 10 **do**
$$s := s + A[i]$$
Q. E. D.

In the second case, the rules applied once give the loop

for j := 1 **step** 1 **until** 30 **do**
$$s := s + sigma(B[i,j], i, 20)$$

Applying the rules again, and remembering that local variables can be systematically renamed we get (not in strict ALGOL!)

$$s := 0;$$
for j := 1 **step** 1 **until** 30 **do**
$$s := s + \textbf{result of}$$
$$sl := 0;$$
for i := 1 **step** 1 **until** 20 **do**
$$sl := sl + B[i,j];$$
$$\textbf{result} := sl$$

Again, Q. E. D.

Since the actual parameter is evaluated every time it is used in the body, rather than just once on entry, it is not perhaps surprising that apart from ALGOL 60, and ALGOL W, no other language uses this technique. If call-by-name were to be replaced in ALGOL 60 by call-by-reference, the only casualty would be Jensen's device, and only compulsively ingenious programmers would regret that, since whenever Jensen's device is used there is almost certainly a faster way of achieving the same end.

It is of interest to note that although ALGOL 68 does not permit call-by-name it is still possible to obtain the same effect. The key to this trick is to observe that a name-parameter has much in common with a function parameter. In fact a name parameter that is not an expression is treated in the evaluation exactly as if it were a function. Thus if in ALGOL 60 we have a name parameter that is an integer, e.g.

procedure $q(k)$;
integer k;
.....

in ALGOL 68 the parameter becomes a **proc** of mode **ref int** thus

proc q = (**proc ref int** k): ...

and likewise the actual parameter: instead of $q(a[i])$ in ALGOL 68 we have

$q($**proc ref int** : $a[i])$

and hand over an anonymous function. This will be evaluated each time it is used, giving the same effect as call-by-name. For completeness we give the ALGOL 68 equivalent of the procedure sigma, the epitome of Jensen's device: (cf. page 62)

$$\textbf{proc } sigma = (\textbf{proc real } a, \textbf{ ref int } i, \textbf{ int } n) \textbf{ real:}$$
$$\textbf{begin real } s := 0;$$
$$\textbf{for } k \textbf{ from } 1 \textbf{ to } n \textbf{ do}$$
$$\textbf{begin } i := k; s := s + a \textbf{ end};$$
$$s$$
$$\textbf{end};$$

When called e.g. as $sigma(A[i], i, 10)$, the $A[i]$ is coerced to a procedure: this device is called "proceduring".

Many variants of the parameter-passing mechanisms can be found. For example some Fortran compilers use a hybrid system that resembles ALGOL call-by-value in that a local variable is created which is initialised to the actual value. However, at the end of the sub-program the current value of the local variable is used to update the actual parameter. This can produce some interesting effects arising from the delayed action updating, and the effect is uncertain if the actual parameter is a constant or an expression. (The same system is provided in ALGOL-W as "call-by-value-result".) The attraction is one of implementation: it is often more efficient to be able to treat the formal parameters as local variables thus maintaining a well-defined context for the routine, rather than to repeatedly address out-of-context using a reference provided as a parameter. (This property of "locality" is particularly important in a virtual-memory system.)

Attributes of a function/routine

When we declare a function or routine we are introducing a new name that is associated with a (constant) function body as its value. What are the attributes associated with such a variable? They comprise a specification of the type (mode) of each formal parameter and of the result (if a function), together with the method of parameter passing (if not implicit). Some languages, notably PL/I, require a recursive function to have the attribute RECURSIVE explicitly specified. This information about the parameters may be required to permit checking of consistency between formal and actual parameters: it also facilitates independent compiling of sub-programs.

Notation in this area is inconsistent. ALGOL 60 and PL/I give the type of the formal parameters by separate declarations, e.g.

(ALGOL 60) **real procedure** $f(x,y)$;
                real x,y;

(PL/I) F: PROC (X, Y) RETURNS (FLOAT(8));
          DCL (X, Y) FLOAT DECIMAL (8);

In ALGOL 60 the heading becomes more verbose if mode of call has to be specified, e.g.

    procedure $f(x,y)$;
    value x; **real** x, y;

(Call-by-name is assumed unless specified otherwise.)

Much more elegant and readable is the ALGOL W convention illustrated by the following example:

PROCEDURE F(REAL VALUE X, REAL RESULT Y)

Similar variability is found in the specification of the value for a function. ALGOL 60 and ALGOL W regard the type of result as defining a class of functions, e.g.

    real procedure $g(x,y)$

signifies a function with a real value. FORTRAN follows a similar rule, but also allows the type of result to be inferred from the function name. PL/I allows a default assumption from the name, or alternatively allows an explicit specification, e.g.

CART: PROC (R, THETA) RETURNS (COMPLEX);

Far and away the most consistent and elegant system is found in ALGOL 68. Consider the simple definition that follows:

    proc $fourthroot$ = (**real** x) **real**: $sqrt(sqrt(x))$;

This is a declaration of a **proc** (the abbreviation is compulsory and objectionable) called fourthroot. The first component on the right of the "=" specifies that this function has an argument x which is a **real** value, and produces a **real** value as a result. Following the colon is the procedure body, in this case just an expression. The argument x is transmitted as a value in the manner discussed earlier. When the procedure is called its argument must be something that is capable of yielding a real value, and this conditions the evaluation of the argument in the same way that the evaluation of the right-hand side of an assignment is conditioned by the quantity required by the left-hand side.

The procedure would of course fail if its argument were negative. We might alternatively want to define a procedure with two arguments x,y such that if $x>0$ the fourth root of x is stored in y and the value of the procedure is **true**, whilst if $x<0$ the value of the procedure is to be **false**, and y left unchanged. A possible definition is

> **proc** *fourthroot* = (**real** x, **ref real** y) **bool**:
> (**if** $x>0$ **then false else**
> y := *sqrt*(*sqrt* (x)); **true fi**);

As before, parameter x is a **real** value; however, since y occurs on the left of an assignment in the procedure body the argument provided must yield a reference to a real variable, thus the value transmitted must be a reference (**fi** marks the end of the **if** clause. Note the mixture of commands and expressions.)

A point on which language designers differ is the extent to which the parameters actually passed to a procedure are consistent with the specification of the formal parameters. ALGOL 60 does not require a specification of formal parameters, so checking is not possible. However, many implementations require specification and perform checks. FORTRAN is similarly deficient: since the only form of parameter passing is to pass an address (in machine terms) the user can get away with murder. For example, if a formal parameter is an array, the corresponding actual parameter can be an array of different rank and size from the formal parameter. In PL/I any discrepancy between the attributes of the formal parameters and the corresponding actual parameters causes the parameter to be called by value, even though it may be a simple name which would *a priori* indicate call by reference.

Some languages, notably POP-2, allow a function to be called with fewer (or more) actual parameters than there are formal parameters in the definition. This opens the door to low cunning and trickery of a reprehensible kind. (This is not to say that a procedure with a variable number of parameters is not a useful - though rarely provided - facility, merely that if it is provided it should be done in a sanitary manner. One possibility is to define a function with a single formal parameter that can be replaced by a list when the function is called.)

Local and non-local variables

Most languages (with the notable exception of COBOL) permit the use of local variables, that is variables that have a meaning only whilst the function body in which they are defined is being executed. They may in consequence clash in name with variables used outside the function body: this is an essential facility if we are to be able to write programs in a modular fashion, i.e. defining functions (routines) that can be written without knowing the precise context in which they will be used (and which can be used in more than one context).

In FORTRAN the situation is simple: variables in a sub-program are local unless they are declared to be in a COMMON block. In ALGOL 60 local variables are declared at the beginning of the block which forms the procedure body, and the usual scope rules apply i.e. for variables not declared at the head of the block, examine the next enclosing block and so on. A difficulty arises in that this is a static, textual nesting, whilst at run-time there is also a dynamic nesting of procedure calls. Thus if we have an expression

$$a + f(b) + c$$

the context (environment) when we come to obey the call of $f(b)$ is not the same as the context in which f was declared. The meaning of a, b and c is resolved by looking at the declarations at the heads of the statically enclosing blocks, but for any names occurring in the body of the function f it is necessary to examine the declarations of the blocks enclosing the definition of f. The compiler must therefore arrange that at run-time two independent chains are maintained: a static chain linking textually nested declarations, and a dynamic chain linking the procedures that have been called but not yet completed. (In practice the static chain is usually implemented by a special mechanism called the "display vector" in the interests of efficiency. The Burroughs B6700 and related machines have this mechanism built into the hardware.)

The behaviour of local variables depends on the storage allocation strategy dictated by the language. If recursion is forbidden, then static allocation can be used. A corollary is that local variables retain their values between calls. If the language dictates the use of dynamic (stack) allocation a new set of local variables will be created for each invocation of the procedure. Thus recursion is possible, but the value of local variables from previous invocations is lost. There is arguably a need for a kind of local variable that is only accessible when it is in scope (i.e. during execution of the procedure) but retains its value whilst it is out of scope. Such a variable is often called an **own** variable, because it "belongs to" the procedure in which it is declared. In PL/I the effect can be obtained by specifying STATIC storage. (Strictly, INTERNAL

STATIC. The attribute EXTERNAL STATIC gives the same effect as FORTRAN COMMON storage, except that association is by name rather than by position, as in a COMMON block.) In ALGOL 60 the qualifier **own** is used. Trouble arises with **own arrays**, and these are not usually implemented. The difficulty arises if the **own array** has dynamic bounds. Consider the following:

> **begin**   **real** a;
>   **real procedure** $f(x, n)$; **value** x, n; **real** x; **integer** n;
>   **begin own real array** $vec[1:n]$;
>
>   ...
>   ...
>   **end** f;
>
> ...
> $a := f(3.2, 100)$; $...a := f(3, 150)$; ...
> **end**

The evaluation of f involves a local array vec whose size is determined by the parameter n. Since vec is an **own** variable its value must be preserved between calls of f, but how can the value be preserved if the array changes size between calls? Evidently, the **own** concept is only of use for scalar variables.

Further ramifications are possible. Consider the following ALGOL program.

> **begin real** a, b;
> $a := 41$;
>
>   ....
>   **begin real procedure** $f(x)$;
>   **real** x; $f := x + a$
>
>   ....
> $a := 3$;
> L1: $b := f(4)$;
>
>   ....
>   **end**
>
> ....
>   **end**

What is the value of b at label L1: 7 or 45? This depends on whether the a in the definition of f takes the value it had when the function was defined, or the value it has when the function is called.

To analyse this situation, we note that a variable occurring in a function body must belong to one of three groups, the formal parameters, the local variables, and the free (or global) variables. The formal parameters and the local variables are entirely private to the function, in the sense that they do not depend on anything outside the function body (except for the initial values of the formal parameters, supplied at the call). We call such variables *bound variables*. Thus the communication between a function and the outside world is channelled through two lists, the *bound variable list* (BVL) and the *free variable list* (FVL). The question we have to ask is, at function definition do we record references or values in the FVL? If we record references, the free variables will take the current values at the time of call, whilst storing values in the FVL will make the free variables take the values current at the time of the function definition.

Few if any languages give an explicit choice to the programmer in this respect. POP-2 provides a facility which effectively provides the choice. In POP-2 the FVL holds references so it is the current value of a free variable that is used. If it is desired to get the effect of using the definition-time value, then we make the free variable an extra formal parameter and "freeze" its value by the device of "partial application".

Thus the above example would be written

```
FUNCTION F2 X A1;
COMMENT NOTE THAT A1 IS A FORMAL PARAMETER;
X + A1;
END
VARS F; F2(%A%) → F;
```

The effect of F2(%A%) is to partially apply F2 by freezing the value of its second parameter to the now current value of A, thus producing a function of one less variable that is assigned as the value of F.

The above discussion has assumed the normal rules of block structure, so that a non-local reference is resolved by examining its context in the static or lexicographic nesting of blocks. APL does not have statically nested blocks, but does permit functions to have local variables. References within a function to non-local quantities are resolved in the context of the dynamic nesting of function calls at run-time. To achieve this, the value associated with a name is held in a push down list, so that a new declaration temporarily suppresses the previous value(s). This can lead to some unexpected effects: for example, consider the following definitions in a system where non-local references are resolved in the dynamic context.

(a) **function** $f(x)$;
$x + y$;
function $g(r)$;
$f(r)$;

and
(b)   **function** $f(x)$;
       $x + y$;
       function $g(y)$;
       $f(y)$;

If y has the value 3, definitions (a) will make $g(4) = 7$ as
expected, but definitions (b) will give $g(4) = 8$. This is because
the call $g(4)$ establishes a variable y with value 4, then calls f
with argument 4. f uses the current value (4) for its free
variable y, and so arrives at the unexpected result.

   Finally we should mention the PL/I solution, which is to
require non-local variables to be explicitly declared as
EXTERNAL, e.g.

DECLARE Z COMPLEX EXTERNAL;

Such external variables are allocated static storage (i.e. not on
the stack): they are to all intents and purposes the same as
FORTRAN COMMON variables, except that they are matched
by name, whereas items in a FORTRAN COMMON block are
matched by position in the block.

Block structure and independent compiling of functions

A static block structure is a powerful conceptual aid, since it
allows the user to define one piece of program to be part of
another program. However, at first sight it has the practical
disadvantage that a program has to be compiled as a whole. It
is possible to alleviate this by observing that a function (procedure) that does not use any free variables is essentially a
self-contained object. PL/I in its definition, and most ALGOL
60 implementations as a matter of pragmatism, allow such a
procedure to be compiled independently. In the program which
is to use it, such a procedure must be declared as **external**, and
all its attributes may have to be given either explicitly or by
default, e.g. in ICL 1900 Algol we might have the declarations

```
begin
procedure datenow; external;
real procedure sum (i,a,b,r);
value a,b; integer i,a,b;
real P; algol;
  . . .
  . . .
```

The basic symbol **external** indicates a procedure written in
assembly code; **algol** indicates a separately compiled Algol
procedure.

70

Generic functions

We have noted earlier that operators such as +, –, etc. are poly-morphic, i.e. their meaning depends on the kind of operands (real, integer, etc.). A function with the same property is called a *generic* function. In PL/I the built-in functions (square root, exponential, sine, cosine, etc.) are generic, thus we can write SIN(X) whatever the attributes of X (as long as it is numeric!). In contrast, FORTRAN requires a different name for each variant of a generic function, e.g. SQRT, CSQRT, DSQRT, etc. (There is no ISQRT, which causes much sorrow to the innocent who writes SQRT(N). The apparently irrelevant error message that most systems give merely adds insult to injury.) PL/I allows the user to define his own generic functions. For example, it is possible to write

```
DCL   F  GENERIC
      (FSHORT ENTRY(FLOAT(6)) RETURNS
      (FLOAT(6)),
      FLONG ENTRY(FLOAT(16)) RETURNS
      (FLOAT(16)));
```

Following this declaration, a call of F will be treated as a call of FSHORT if its argument has attributes FLOAT(6), and as a call of FLONG if the argument has attributes FLOAT(16). (FSHORT and FLONG are of course defined elsewhere.) Thus we have a function F that works for "single precision" and for "double precision" arguments. However, there are concealed traps: the call F(3.14) would be rejected since the argument in this case has neither the attributes FLOAT(6) nor the attributes FLOAT(16).

ALGOL 68 does not allow definition of generic functions by the user, and the built-in functions have distinctive names, e.g. sqrt, long sqrt, long long sqrt, etc. However, operators in ALGOL 68 are generic, and the user can define his own generic operators (see the section on operator definition later in this Chapter).

Notation for calling functions and routines

Functions and routines are usually called using prefix notation, thus: $f(x,y)$. A function call appears as a component of an expression: a routine call is a statement in its own right. In FORTRAN and PL/I (for example) a routine call requires the explicit word CALL thus:

```
CALL  F(X,Y);
```

In ALGOL 60 on the other hand, a routine is called merely by writing the name with its parameters, thus:

$$f(x,y);$$

(In fact, the ALGOL 60 syntax does not distinguish calls of functions and routines. It is permissible (though pointless) to write "sin(x);" as a statement on its own. It will cause sin(x) to be evaluated, placed on the stack, and lost.)

It is interesting to observe that when prefix notation is used, almost all languages write the actual parameters as a simple list of items separated by commas. No high-level language uses the key-word parameters commonly found in macro-assemblers. ALGOL 60 makes a feeble gesture in this direction in that it allows the comma that separates parameters to be replaced by the sequence

$$)<letter\ string>\ :($$

This makes it possible to use constructions such as

procedure $f(x)$ *is the input and the output is*: (y)

instead of **procedure** $f(x,y)$. The same kind of construction is possible in a procedure call, but this can be most misleading since the letter string has no semantic significance: association between formal and actual parameters is on a purely positional basis. Thus, given the procedure heading above, the casual user might be tempted to call the procedure f in the following way:

$$f(z)\ is\ the\ output\ and\ the\ input\ is:\ (w)$$

This is identical in meaning to $f(z,w)$ so that z will be associated with the formal parameter x (the input), and w with y (the output): this is presumably not what the user intended, and detection of the error may be very difficult.

Although used almost universally, prefix notation is not the only one available for function calls. POP-2 allows postfix notation in which $f(x)$ becomes $x.f.$ This fits into the POP-2 philosophy in a self-consistent way: "x" means "evaluate x and put value on the stack", and "$.f$" means "apply f to the argument(s) on the stack, leaving result(s) on the stack. The dot notation removes the plethora of closing brackets that plagues list-processing systems, thus

$$hd(tl(tl(hd(hd(x))))) $$

becomes

$$x.hd.hd.tl.tl.hd$$

It sometimes makes predicates easier to read,

e.g.   **if** *x.isvalid* . . . . ,
rather than   **if** *isvalid*(x) . . .

and it is particularly useful in data structure manipulation (see Chapter 5). (It also opens the way to immoral tricks such as defining a function with a certain number of arguments, and calling it with a different number of arguments.)

Functions and routines with no arguments present some complications. FORTRAN and PL/I permit routines to have no parameters; FORTRAN insists that functions must have at least one parameter, PL/I allows functions without parameters provided that the name is declared with attribute ENTRY for the block(s) in which it occurs.

ALGOL 60, ALGOL 68 and POP-2 permit functions with no arguments, but differ in the way they deal with them. In ALGOL 60 a function with no arguments is called just by writing its name. (Since procedures must be declared before they are used there is no ambiguity.) This facility can be used to advantage in ALGOL programs to make them "self documenting".

For example, suppose we have a program that starts with a number of initialising statements. We define a procedure to contain all these thus:

> **procedure** *initialise variables*;
> **begin**
>   <*initialising statements*>
> **end**

Our main program can then start with the line

> *initialise variables*;

which is self-explanatory. (Note that we cannot do this in FORTRAN because of the necessity of the CALL statement.) Following this technique, we can produce a self-annotating "driver" program that might look as follows.

> *initialise variables*;
> *read data*;
> *main calculation*;
> *print relevant values*;

Each line is a call for a procedure with no parameters.

Similar clarity can be gained by using Boolean functions of no variables in conditional statements. We might for example write

> **if** *singular point* **then** . . . . . . **else** . . . . . .

where "singular point" is a Boolean procedure that may be

quite elaborate.

In ALGOL 60 we can make use of the fact that a type-procedure with no arguments looks exactly like a variable in an expression. We can achieve the effect of an ALGOL 68 constant definition by using this feature. Thus suppose we declare

> **real procedure** *pi*;
> *pi* := 3.1415926536;

then we can use *pi* as a constant, e.g.

> *z* := *sin*(*theta* * (*pi*/180.0))

but if we attempt to change the value of *pi* by an assignment, e.g.

> *pi* := 22/7

we shall get an error halt since we cannot assign to a procedure. Other applications of this ingenious device will be given later.

In POP-2 a call of a function with no arguments is indicated by empty brackets, thus: itemread( ). This is necessary because a function name on its own stands for the function itself, which is an object in its own right. In ALGOL 68, although functions can be manipulated, the ALGOL 60 notation is used. The system determines by context whether it is the function or its value that is required. Thus, suppose *random* is a function with no arguments that produces a real result, and we have the declarations

> **real** *x*;
> **proc real** *p*;

then   *x* := *random*;

will cause the procedure *random* to be evaluated, because a **real** value is required in the context, whereas

> *p* := *random*;

causes *p* to become a procedure with an effect identical to *random*: in other words the actual procedure body has been assigned. We refer to the automatic evaluation in the first case as "de-proceduring": it is akin to the dereferencing discussed in Chapter 3.

Operators

Another possibility for a function of two arguments is to place the operation between the arguments. (In APL this is mandatory.)

It is not always realised that an infix operator like '+' is just another function name: the syntax analyser needs to know the precedence (except in APL), but that is the only difference. For this facility to be useful, however, it is desirable to allow non-alphabetic function names (as does POP-2).

The difference between an operator and a function is thus essentially a syntactic one of the way the arguments are presented. A function always takes its arguments from the stack, so that the POP-2 definition

```
FUNCTION HCF  M  N;
<body>
END;
```

is equivalent to

```
FUNCTION HCF;
VARS M  N;
→N; →M;
<body>
END;
```

In the same way, when a dyadic operator ϕ is encountered in the context $a \phi b$, the action is to load a and b on the stack and enter the function definition associated with the operation ϕ.

Suppose that we have defined in POP-2 a conventional function called HCF. If we make extensive use of the HCF function, we might wish to be able to use an infix operator, say ££, so that we could write A ££ B instead of HCF(A,B). (This is not just a matter of taste: extensive use of prefix notation leads to a proliferation of brackets.) To do this, we would follow the function definition by the lines

```
VARS OPERATOR 2 ££;
HCF → NONOP ££;
```

This declares ££ to be an operator of precedence 2 (see below) and assigns HCF as the value of that variable. Remember that HCF without arguments refers to the function, not the result of applying it to its operands. (Note also the use of NONOP before ££ – we do not wish ££ to be treated as an operator in this context, just as a name.)

££ was defined as an operation "of precedence 2". The precedence of an operation determines the order in which things get done in the absence of brackets. For example, if we write

```
A + B ££ C + D
```

do we mean (A+B) ££ (C+D) or A+(B ££ C)+D? In POP-2 the normal arithmetic operations have precedences:

```
+, − 5
*, / 4
↑   3
```

Low numbers count high (precedence is a relative ordering, not an absolute value) so that making ££ an operation of precedence 2 we ensure that it is done before any other arithmetic operation.

ALGOL 68 allows a similar form of operator definition. The above example would become:

> **priority hcf** = 9;
> c *high numbers indicate high precedence*
>   *in ALGOL 68* c
> **op hcf** = (**int** *m,n*) **int**:
> <*body of procedure declaration*>

However, in ALGOL 68 we have a further source of complication. Since it is an L-typed language, an operator declaration will be tied to particular types of argument. Thus if we declare

> **op max** = (**real** *x,y*) **real**:
>   if $x > y$ then x else y **fi**;

we have an infix operator that only works for **real** arguments. We can if we wish define generic or polymorphic operators thus:

> **op max** = (**real** *x,y*) **real**: if $x > y$ then x else y **fi**,
>   **max** = (**int** *i,j*) **int**: if $i > j$ then i else j **fi**,
>   **max** = (**long real** *x,y*) **long real**: if $x > y$ then x
>   else y **fi**;

We now have an infix operator **max** that is defined for **int**, **real**, and **long real** arguments. It would be possible if we so desired to define **max** also for character strings, perhaps defining it in the sense of alphabetic ordering. This would open the way to writing a sort procedure based on the exchange method that would work for **ints**, **reals**, **long reals** and **strings**.

A particularly useful application of this feature is the ability to define operators whose arguments are arrays or structures. Thus it is possible to define the operator * so that if it appears between two vectors its value is their inner product. Then if x is **real**, and $v1$, $v2$ are vectors of **reals** of the same size, provided we get the precedence right we can write $x*v1*v2$ and get the value $x * \Sigma v1[i] * v2[i]$.

i

"Left-hand" functions

Consider the function

$$f(b,x,y) = \textbf{if } b \textbf{ then } x \textbf{ else } y$$

In the light of our previous discussion we can give a clear interpretation of the following use of the function:

$$f(b,x,y) := z$$

Provided that the function is given references for x and y, it will yield a reference and is therefore a respectable thing to find on the left of an assignment. But consider another function

$$Bit(i,k)$$

which selects the i'th bit in the binary representation of the integer k. We can readily see what is meant by the constructions

$$p := Bit(j,n)$$
$$\text{and } Bit(j,n) := p$$

but the operations to be carried out in the two cases are entirely different. (Any function which includes a data structure in its domain has this property of defining two separate operations – a *selector* when used in an "R-context" and an *updater* when used in an "L-context".) "Left-hand" functions do not occur very commonly in languages. PL/I includes some built-in left-hand functions. For example, the function SUBSTR(S,N,M) has as its value in a right-hand context the substring of length M starting at position N in the string S. SUBSTR can also be used in a left-hand context, e.g. SUBSTR(S,3,2) = 'PQ', and in this context it is called a "pseudo-variable". Other pseudo-variables in PL/I include the functions REAL and IMAG used in manipulating the components of complex numbers, e.g.

    DCL Z COMPLEX
    . . .
    . . .
    REAL(Z) = 3.14

The POP-2 approach to left-hand functions is interesting and instructive. The construction $z \rightarrow f(x_1, \ldots . x_k)$ is treated as a euphemism for the call of a routine $f'(z,x_1, \ldots x_k)$, where f' is the *updater* of the function f, associated with f by the operation $f' \rightarrow updater\,(f)$. Although the formal definition of the language allows an updater to be associated with any function, in practice it can only be done if the function operates on a data structure, since otherwise the call $f'(z,x_1, \ldots x_k)$ could not actually change anything outside its own local variables.

An example may help to make this clear. POP-2 provides a built-in data structure called a *pair*, which is made up of two components, the *front* and the *back*. If *p* is a pair, we might define a function to determine the smaller of its two components as follows:

> **function** *smaller p*;
> **if** *front*(*p*) < *back*(*p*) **then** *front*(*p*) **else** *back*(*p*) **close**
> **end**;

We might well want to use this in a "left-hand" context, e.g.

> 0 → *smaller*(*p*);

To do this we define an updater as follows:

> **function** *sm z p*;
> **if** *front*(*p*) < *back*(*p*) **then** *z* → *front*(*p*)
>   **else** *z* → *back*(*p*) **close**
> **end**;

and relate the two by *sm* → *updater*(*smaller*). Then the assignment 0 → *smaller*(*p*) is treated as *sm*(0,*p*) which evidently has the desired effect.

It might seem that since ALGOL 68 manipulates references explicitly, left-hand functions would follow automatically, being simply functions whose value is a reference. However, we encounter a difficulty. Suppose we define

> **proc** *smaller* = (**ref real** *x,y*)**real**: **if** *x* < *y* **then** *x*
>   **else** *y* **fi**;

then 'smaller' can only be used in a context where a **real** value is required: when called it leaves a **real** value on the stack. (The parameters *x* and *y* need not be **ref real**, of course: **real** would suffice.) If we now want to convert this into a left-hand function, we might be tempted to change it as follows:

> **proc smaller** = (**ref real** *x,y*)**ref real**:
>   **begin ref real** *c* := **if** *x* < *y* **then** *x* **else** *y* **fi**; *c* **end**

Superficially this appears to work. *x* and *y* will be dereferenced for the comparison, but since the mode of *c* is **ref ref real**, the conditional will yield a **ref real** to be assigned. However, the space for *c* is produced by a local generator, and the scope of *c* ends at the **end** of the function. We would therefore be passing on a reference to space that was out of scope, with unknown consequences. To get round this we have to make *c* global by using "heap" storage. The ALGOL 68 heap is a dynamically administered storage area: space is allocated as requested, and when no more is available a garbage collection mechanism recovers space that is not accessible via any current references. Its use is therefore not conducive to efficiency. To get the effect required we would write

> **proc** *smaller* = (**ref real** x,y)**ref real**:
>   **begin ref real** c = **heap real**;
> c := **if** $x < y$ **then** x **else** y **fi**; c
>   **end**

The function now generates a reference to a **heap real** that can safely be passed out of scope.

Functions as data objects

If we write a program to do numerical quadrature it will fall clearly into two parts: one which is common to all integrations and one which is specialised to the particular function being integrated. Thus if we write (in some high-level language) a general purpose quadrature routine, we shall wish to give it as parameters the upper and lower limits of the integration, and a function to evaluate the integrand. Here is an example of treating a function as a data object, since it is being passed as a parameter to another function in much the same way as a number.

Most languages provide this facility (e.g. the EXTERNAL statement in FORTRAN, **procedure** parameters in ALGOL 60, the ENTRY attribute for parameters in PL/I), but this is generally the only circumstance in which functions are treated as data objects. A recent trend in languages is to promote functions to the status of "first-class" objects, by putting them on exactly the same footing as any other data object. POP-2 and ALGOL 68 are examples of this trend.

In POP-2 a variable can take a function as its value. Thus

> SIN(X) → Y;

assigns the value of sin(X) – a numerical quantity – whereas

> SIN → Z;

makes the actual function body of SIN the value of Z. It is then legitimate to write

> Z(X) → Y;

More useful would be a conditional assignment, e.g.

> IF B THEN SIN ELSE COS CLOSE → TRIG;

Another example of a variable taking a function for a value

arises in passing parameters to functions. For example, to evaluate

$$\int_A^B F(X)dX$$

we might define a function QUAD(A,B,F) which would expect numerical values to replace A and B, and a function to replace F. Thus to evaluate

$$\int_0^{\pi/2} cos\ x\ dx$$

we would write

QUAD(0.0, 1.5708, COS)

and to evaluate

$$\int_0^1 \frac{dx}{1+x^2}$$

we would write (in POP-2)

FUNCTION INTEGRAND X;1/(1+X*X) END;
QUAD(0.0,1.0,INTEGRAND);

Rather than define the function INTEGRAND, we might find it more convenient to write a "function constant" as the argument of QUAD in the same way that the constant upper and lower limits are written explicitly. (Apart from anything else, this saves us the bother of inventing unique names for what are essentially anonymous functions.) To do this we would write

QUAD(0.0,1.0,LAMBDA X;1/(1+X*X) END);

LAMBDA is used to introduce a function constant: the notation LAMBDA X;...END can be read as "the function of X whose definition is ...". Note that X is a dummy variable. The same notation can be used to define functions – the following are equivalent definitions.

(i)   FUNCTION FOURTHROOT X;
      SQRT(SQRT(X)) END;
(ii) VARS FOURTHROOT;
      LAMBDA X;SQRT(SQRT(X)) END → FOURTHROOT;

The lambda notation also opens up a very important new possibility, the ability to define a function whose value is itself a function. Thus suppose we define

```
FUNCTION AD X;
LAMBDA Y; Y + X END;
END
```

then the value of AD(3) is a function which will add 3 to its argument. However, there are dangers. If we make the call AD(Z) then we produce another function which has a reference to Z built into its definition. But we can now use this function in a context where Z is undefined – in a hole in its extent. (We can get round this by the use of partial application.)

In ALGOL 68, procedures are "first-class objects". A **proc** is an object that can be manipulated in the same way as any other. In particular, it can be passed as an argument to another **proc**. Thus a quadrature function could be declared as

> **proc** *Gauss* = (**real** *lowerlimit, upperlimit,*
> **proc** (**real**) **real** *fn*) **real**:
> **begin** .... **end**

The specification indicates that the formal parameter *fn* must be replaced by a **proc** that takes one **real** argument and produces a **real** result.

Indeed, a definition

> **proc** *g* = ...

is in fact a declaration of a variable *g* whose value will be a piece of program with a constant initialisation for *g*. (Cf. **real pi** = 3.14159.) Thus by using the other form of initialisation we could declare a **proc** whose body could be changed later, or we can declare a variable as a **proc** without giving it a body. (We must however specify its argument structure and the type of its results.) For example,

> **proc** (**real**) **real** *p*;

declares *p* as the name of a procedure that takes a real parameter and a real result, but does not specify the procedure body. (This would obviously be of use in designing a general-purpose package into which the user is going to insert some special procedures.) Once a **proc** has been declared in this way it can subsequently be given a value by assignment. Thus

> *p* := *sqrt*

would be a valid (though probably not very useful) assignment. More useful would be assignment of an explicit procedure body, e.g.

p := (**real** x) **real**: *sqrt(sqrt(x))*;

(Observe that the right-hand side of this assignment is a lambda expression in an unusual notation.)

In the same way that we can declare a "**ref real**" variable whose value is the name of a real quantity, so we can declare a **ref proc** variable whose value is the name of a **proc**. For example,

ref proc (**real**) **real** g;

declares g to be the name of a place where we can store the name of a **proc** that takes a real argument and takes a real result.

Fun with functions

We have already remarked that in ALGOL 60 a call of a procedure with no parameters looks like an occurrence of a simple variable. This feature of the language is exploited in the following example of vector algebraic manipulation, due to Dr K. V. Roberts of the Culham Laboratory. It is extracted from a system in which the equation

$$\frac{\partial B}{\partial t} = curl(V \times B) + curl(\eta \ curl \ B)$$

becomes the program statement

```
AB[C,Q] := B + DT*(CURL(CROSS(V,B)) +
          CURL(ETA*CURL(B)));
```

(In a language that allows left-hand functions and user-defined operators, the correspondence could be made even closer.)

We consider the solution of a partial differential equation in three space-dimensions, and in order to use finite difference approximations we set up a three-dimensional mesh. There are NI, NJ, NK mesh points in the x, y, z directions respectively, and to deal with edge effects an extra layer of guard points is included outside each boundary. A point (x, y, z) can now be referred to in terms of its coordinates (i, j, k) in the mesh, the relation being

```
X = I*DS    (0 ≤ I < NI–1)
Y = J*DS    (0 ≤ J < NJ–1)
Z = K*DS    (0 ≤ K < NK–1)
```

Including the guard points the total number of points is

```
SIZE = PI*PJ*PK
```

where PI = NI + 2, etc.

When setting up a computer program it is convenient to map this mesh onto a linear array, and to label the mesh points with a single suffix Q which lies between 1 and SIZE. It is easily seen that

$$Q = 1 + (I + 1) + (J + 1)*PI + (K + 1)*PI*PJ$$

Now suppose we are interested in a scalar function F defined over the mesh. We represent this by an array, and use a parameter-less procedure as a shorthand for the array reference thus:

> **real array** AF[1:SIZE];
> **real procedure** F; F := AF[Q];

Similarly for a vector function V we define

> **real array** AV[1:3,1:SIZE];
> **real procedure** V; V := AV[C,Q];

Here C is a global integer that will take the value 1, 2 or 3.

It will often be convenient to think in terms of the physical variables X, Y and Z, although all operations are in fact carried out using the indices I, J, K that act as coordinates in the mesh. To do this we can define a further set of parameterless functions. We first define some auxiliary functions to disentangle I, J and K from Q.

> **integer procedure** *kplus*1; *kplus*1 := (Q−1)÷(PI*PJ);
> **integer procedure** *jplus*1; *jplus*1 := (Q−1−*kplus*1*PI*PJ)÷PI;
> **integer procedure** *iplus*1; *iplus*1 := (Q−1−(*jplus*1+*kplus*1*PJ)*PI)

We then define

> **real procedure** X; X := (*iplus*1−1)*DS;
> **real procedure** Y; Y := (*jplus*1−1)*DS;
> **real procedure** Z; Z := (*kplus*1−1)*DS;

As an example of the use of these procedures, consider the problem of setting up initial values on the mesh. We define a procedure to do this as follows:

> **procedure** *set scalar* (A,F); **real array** A; **real** F;
> **begin**
> **for** I := 0 **step** 1 **until** NI−1 **do**
> **for** J := 0 **step** 1 **until** NJ−1 **do**
> **for** K := 0 **step** 1 **until** NK−1 **do**
>   **begin** Q := I+2+PI*(J+1+(K+1)*PJ);A [Q] := F; **end**;
>
> **comment** *note extensive use of global variables*;
> **end**;

We can now write calls to this procedure like

set scalar (AF, X**2+Y**2+Z**2);
or   *set scalar* (AF, **if** X+Y > 2 **then** 1 **else** 0);

Note what is happening. Set scalar computes Q for each grid point by setting the global variables I, J and K. When the final assignment is made, the second argument is evaluated (it was called by name): it involves X, Y and Z which are evaluated in terms of the current settings of I, J and K. Note that this is a situation where call by name is particularly useful, since it allows an expression as an actual parameter and evaluates it each time round.

To implement more complicated operations we need a few more auxiliary procedures. Recall that a global variable C determines which component of a vector we are currently dealing with. We first introduce operators RP and RM (rotate plus and rotate minus respectively) that have the effect of permuting the suffix of a vector component. (Thus if C=2 then RF(A) gives A_3 and RM(A) gives A_1.) The definition of RP is

real procedure RP(A); **real** A;
begin C := CP[C]; RP := A; C := CM[C]; **end**

Here CP is the vector 2, 3, 1 and CM the vector 3, 1, 2 . Note the use of a reversible side effect in the procedure. Remember also that when called the argument A will be a parameterless procedure defined as an element of a 2-dimensional array, so that changing C then assigning RP := A will pick up the appropriate component. We can now define

real procedure *sigma*(F); **real** F; *sigma* :=
   F + RP(F) + RM(F);

and finally the dot product

real procedure *dot* (A,B); **real** A,B;
dot := *sigma*(A*B);

The reader is advised to follow through the working of dot given two vector arguments. Note again how it depends on call-by-name. The extension to define cross, div, grad and curl in a similar manner may not be obvious, but should not be entirely obscure.

5

ARRAYS AND STRUCTURES

Those whom God hath joined together
let no man put asunder.
                The Marriage Service

Compound data items

So far we have been concerned with data items that are
"atomic". That is to say, although they may be complicated
(e.g. function bodies) their internal structure is inaccessible
to the programmer. We now turn to a consideration of
compound data items – aggregates of simple items identified
by a single name. Such aggregates are sometimes manipulated
as a whole, but equally one may want to refer to the individual components. We can immediately divide compound data
items into two classes according to means used to identify
the components.

> *Arrays* are aggregates in which the components are
> identified by their position within the aggregate.
> *Structures* are aggregates in which the components
> are identified by name.

It follows immediately that the components of an array must
all have the same attributes, whereas the components of a
structure can be of mixed types. Another distinction is that
assignment of an array usually results in two copies of the
array coexisting in store, whereas assignment of a structure
results in two pointers to a single copy of the structure. This
is a consequence of the fact that the value of an array is the
collection of values of the components, whilst the value of a
structure is the collection of references to the components.
Structures are a relatively new development in programming
languages (except for the rather rigidly defined structures of
COBOL). Particularly in "scientific" programming, programmers have developed a great skill in doing with arrays jobs
that are better suited to structures. As a general rule we can
assert that arrays are appropriate if the position of the
required components has to be computed at run-time, as in
linear-algebra calculations, whilst structures are appropriate if

the desired element can be specified completely at the time the program is written. In this situation structures are more efficient since the selection operations can be compiled once-and-for-all, whereas the array selection calculations must be performed every time the element is accessed. A less quantifiable benefit is that (given suitable facilities in the language) the data structure can be tailored to match the problem structure, thus simplifying the programmer's task, and reducing the possibility of errors in the logic of the program.

Arrays

Let us now look at arrays in more detail. An element of an array is identified by its position. At the most fundamental level this is a simple count of its linear displacement from the start of the array, but most languages allow the position to be specified in a coordinate system of more than one dimension. Thus an element is identified by a number of indices or subscripts e.g. $A(3, 7, 4)$. The number of subscripts required to identify an element is termed the *dimensionality* of the array, though a mathematician would more properly describe it as the *rank*. (Dimensionality specifies the actual size of the array: its shape is defined by the rank.)

Array storage

Since the actual store of the computer is usually (but not always) a one-dimensional array, arrays are very often held in a contiguous area of store, and given an array reference a *mapping function* is invoked to translate the multiple-subscript form into a position in a linear vector. This is really the province of the compiler writer, but it does (unfortunately) impinge on language design. If we consider a two-dimensional array of m rows and n columns, then we can store it in a one-dimensional area of store in two ways, "by rows" or "by columns". Storage by rows implies the sequence

$A(1,1)$, $A(1,2)$, $A(1,3)$ ... $A(1,n)$, $A(2,1)$, $A(2,2)$ ... ... $A(m,1)$, $A(m,2)$ ... $A(m,n)$

Storage by columns implies the sequence

$A(1,1)$, $A(2,1)$ ... $A(m,1)$, $A(1,2)$, $A(2,2)$ ... ... $A(1,n)$, $A(2,n)$ ... $A(m,n)$

For arrays of higher rank, we can define storage in "row order" or "column order": in row order the *last* index varies most rapidly, whereas in column order the *first* index varies most rapidly.

The way in which arrays are stored should not in general affect a high level language. (It does affect APL, because in that language there are facilities for "reshaping" arrays, i.e. keeping the elements the same but changing the rank and dimensions.) In practice row order is almost universally employed, except for FORTRAN, which specifies column order. The reprehensible thing about ANSI Fortran is that the Standard implies that arrays are stored in column order in a contiguous area of store. Thus if we have DIMENSION A(10,4), then a reference to A(11,1) is legal, and is equivalent to A(1,2). This makes it very difficult to employ array storage techniques (e.g. Iliffe's "codewords") that do not employ contiguous areas of store.

Array declarations

In an L-typed language the declaration of an array must specify its dimensionality. If, as in FORTRAN, the type of the elements can be deduced from the name, and the lower bound of the suffices is implicitly one, then appending the upper bound of the suffices is enough, e.g. DIMENSION A(1), I(4,7). More generally, the type of the elements and the range of the suffices must be declared, e.g. (ALGOL 60) **real array** sums [3:17, −5:4]. ALGOL 68 uses a particularly neat form thus: [3:17, −5:4] **real** sums.

Another way in which implementation is reflected in language design is the question whether an array declaration must specify the dimensions as explicit constants, or whether they can be specified by variables (or expressions), in which case the size of the array will depend on the values of the appropriate variables at the time the declaration is encountered. The restriction to explicit constants is necessary if all storage allocation is to be done at compile-time; the more general approach evidently suits a system in which storage is dynamically allocated. It allows the size of an array to be tailored to a particular case, e.g.

```
begin integer n,m;
read(n); read(m);
   begin real array a[1:n, 1:m];
   . . .
   end
end
```

In ALGOL 68 this would be written in a particularly neat form, thus:

```
    begin int n,m;
    [1:(read(n);n), 1:(read(m);m)] real a;
    . . . . .
    end
```

In an R-typed language we see clearly the two actions of declaring a name and acquiring space to store an array. The latter operation is done by a call to a system function, e.g.

```
    new sums;
    . . .
    . . .
    sums := array [3:17, −5:4];
```

In POP-2 the function that creates an array takes as an additional argument a function that will be used to initialise the array, thus for example

```
    vars ar;
    newarray ([1 3 1 4], lambda i,j; i↑j end);
```

would make *ar* an array of three rows and four columns initialised to

```
    1   1   1    1
    2   4   8   16
    3   9  27   81
```

(We shall in fact see later a much better way of achieving the same effect in POP-2, but the example will suffice.)

Accessing array elements

It is a general feature of languages that include arrays that an element of an array can in most contexts appear wherever a scalar value can appear. (In most contexts, but not all – for example, array elements cannot appear in a Fortran DO statement.) We have to supply the array name and the indices (subscripts). Since these last are integers, it would be logical to allow any expression which evaluates to an integer as a subscript. However, many languages impose restrictions on the form of subscript expressions, the most fierce restrictions being in ANSI Fortran.

If a language allows manipulation of "exotic" objects (e.g. references) as "scalars", it is natural that arrays of such objects should be permitted also. Thus in ALGOL 68 we can write:

```
    [1:3] ref [ ] real w;
```

w is evidently an array of three elements, which are themselves references to arrays of real numbers. If we have also declared three other arrays of real numbers, thus:

$$[1: n1] \textbf{ real } v1;$$
$$[1: n2] \textbf{ real } v2;$$
$$[1: n3] \textbf{ real } v3;$$

we can then write

$$w[1] := v1;$$
$$w[2] := v2;$$
$$w[3] := v3;$$

If $n1 \neq n2 \neq n3$ we have now set up a two-dimensional array that is non-rectangular. We can refer to the third element of $v2$ as $v2[3]$ or $w[2][3]$. The attraction of the latter construction is that the "row" can be selected by computation. We could obtain a highly suggestive notation by defining a **proc** thus:

$$\textbf{proc } ww = (\textbf{int } i, \textbf{ int } j) \textbf{ real} : w[i] \ [j];$$

which would make $ww(i,j)$ equivalent to $w[i] \ [j]$.

This idea can be extended, e.g. to

$$\textbf{ref } [\quad] \textbf{ ref } [\quad] \textbf{ real } xy;$$

which declares a variable xy as the name of a place where we can store the name of a vector of names of vectors of **reals**.

As a further example, note that it is possible in ALGOL 68 to set up a vector of procedures, e.g.

$$[1:4] \textbf{ proc } switch = (\textbf{goto } L1, \textbf{ goto } L2, \textbf{ goto } L3, \textbf{ goto } L4);$$

The syntactic form of an array reference is of some significance. In ALGOL 60 and 68 the subscripts are enclosed in square brackets, e.g. $a[1,7]$. In FORTRAN, PL/I and many other languages they are enclosed in round brackets, e.g. $A(1,7)$. When round brackets are used the syntactic form of an array reference is identical with that of a function call. Whilst this leads to various contortions in FORTRAN compilers, the similarity can be exploited by allowing function calls and array references to be used interchangeably. (An array is essentially a function defined by a table rather than by an algorithm, so the equivalence has some foundation.) The equivalence is easy to include in an R-typed language, and is a useful feature of POP-2. Thus a unit matrix can be defined as a function:

```
function unit i j ;
if i = j then 1 else 0 close
end
```

In a problem involving matrices of 100 rows and 100 columns

the saving in space by defining the unit matrix in this way is evidently appreciable.

Forming sub-sets of arrays

A useful feature of a language is the ability to extract a sub-set of an array. Typical of a simple method is the PL/I facility whereby an asterisk in a subscript position indicates that all possible values of that subscript are to be taken. Thus if A is a two-dimensional array, A(3,*) denotes the third row, and A(*,4) the fourth column. Similar facilities are provided in ALGOL 68 and APL: in both cases the subscript in question is omitted, so that the above examples would become

A[3,] and A[,4] in ALGOL 68
A[3;] and A[;4] in APL.

ALGOL 68 adds the further refinement that if the omitted subscript is the last one the comma may be elided, so that A[3,] can be written A[3]. There are two non-obvious points to be noted

(i)   In APL, if A is an $n \times m$ array, A[3;] is an array of 1 row and m columns, which is not quite the same thing as a one-dimensional array of m elements.

(ii)   In ALGOL 68, something like A[,4] is an array which can itself be indexed, thus A[,4] [3] is equivalent to A[3,4]. In PL/I and APL a subarray formed in this way cannot itself be subscripted.

What we are saying here is that the ALGOL 68 form A[,4] yields an array reference, which may in context be coerced to yield a value by dereferencing, but is also a legitimate object to subscript. In contrast, APL and PL/I yield the value of the array "slice". ALGOL 68 provides another way of extracting a sub-array, called "trimming". Thus if we declare

[1:10] **real** x,

then $x[5:7]$ stands for $(x[5], x[6], x[7])$ and can be used in any context where an array of three **reals** would be appropriate. Once again, the trimmed array can be subscripted (the lower, bound being 1) thus $x[5:7]$ [2] is $x[6]$. (In fact the new lower bound can be set arbitrarily, e.g. $x[5:7$ **at** 10] is indexed from 10 to 12.)

If it is required to name a reference to a sub-array in ALGOL 68, this is done with an identity declaration, e.g.

ref [ ] **real** *subset* = $x[5:7]$.

Anonymous arrays

We have just seen that in ALGOL 68 a sub-array can be sub-scripted. In APL it is permitted to attach a subscript to an *expression* if that expression has an array as its value. Thus

$$2 \quad 3 \quad \rho \quad \text{'NO YES'}$$

is an APL expression that generates a 2 by 3 character array. The expression

$$(2 \quad 3 \quad \rho \quad \text{'NO YES'})[I;]$$

selects a row of the array if I = 1 or I = 2, thus for I = 2 the value of the expression is 'YES'.

Operations on complete arrays

In FORTRAN and ALGOL 60 we can use array elements in place of scalars in expressions, but we cannot in general use the name of the array to stand for the entire aggregate of values. (I/O statements in FORTRAN are an exception to this rule.)

In PL/I, APL and ALGOL 68 we can also assign arrays, thus if A, B have been declared as arrays (of the same shape and size), A = B (or A ← B or A := B as appropriate) will make A a copy of B, i.e. there is an element-by-element assignment. PL/I also allows an assignment A = 0 with the obvious meaning. Other useful PL/I operations on arrays are ANY and ALL, e.g.

$$\text{IF ANY } (A = 0) \ldots$$
$$\text{IF ALL } (A < B) \ldots$$

In all three languages "slices" of an array can be used in assignments: the only requirement is that the arrays on the left and right of the assignment are "conformable", i.e. the same shape and size. For example, in PL/I:

DCL   (10, 10) A . . . . , (10) B . . . ;
. . . .
B = A(I,*);

This is acceptable since A(I,*) is a one-dimensional array of 10 elements. (If you do the same thing in APL you are likely to fall foul of the subtle distinction between a one-dimensional array and a two-dimensional array with only one row. The rank of the former is 1, but the rank of the latter is 2 so they appear not to be conformable.)

The PL/I assignment A = 0 is an example of a more general facility, since PL/I will accept array names as components in a general expression on the right-hand side of an array assignment. Thus if A, B, C are arrays of the same size and shape,

A = 2 * B + C

is a legal PL/I assignment. The interpretation of such a statement is as follows. All arrays within the statement must have the same dimensionality and identical lower and upper bounds. Let these be ℓ_1 :h_1, ℓ_2 :h_2, ... ℓ_n : h_n; and let S1, S2, ... Sn be "private" counters. Then the statement

A = 2 * B + C

is effectively replaced by

LBL: DO S1 = ℓ_1 TO h_1 BY 1;
          DO S2 = ℓ_2 TO h_2 BY 1;
          ....
          DO Sn = ℓ_n TO h_n BY 1;
          A(S1, S2, .. Sn) = 2*B(S1, S2 .. Sn) +
                C(S1, S2, ... Sn)
          END LBL;

This expansion is carried out if an array occurs as a parameter of a built-in function, thus A = ABS(A) has the expected effect if A is an array. However, the expansion does not take place if an array appears as a parameter of a programmer-defined function. The expansion also applies when cross-sections (or "slices") of arrays are used, thus if P. Q are two- and three-dimensional respectively a statement like

P(J,*) = P(1,*) + Q(I,*,J)

is allowed provided that the dimensions conform.

In APL all the elementary operators are defined to operate element-by-element on arrays. This removes a large number of repetition loops from programs (which is fortunate, since APL has no equivalent of the **for** statement). There is, however, an important difference between PL/I and APL in the element-by-element treatment of arrays. Consider the statement

X = X/X(I,J)

In PL/I, after X_{ij} has been changed the **new** value is used in all subsequent operations (because of the way the expansion is done). In the equivalent APL statement

X ← X ÷ X[I,J]

the operations are done on a **copy** of X, which is used to update the original X only when all the arithmetic has been completed.

ALGOL 68 does not automatically extend scalar operators to deal with arrays. However, as we have noted in Chapter 4, an operator can be defined in ALGOL 68 to have differing effects dependent on the mode of its operands. Thus we can define the operator * for one-dimensional arrays to give either an element-by-element product or a scalar product (inner product). Note that the first possibility depends on the fact that in ALGOL 68, unlike most other languages, the value of a function can be an array. We can also define monadic operators on arrays, e.g.

> **op** *abs* = ([1:] **real** *a*1) [1:] **real**:
>   **begin** [1:**upb** *a*1] **real** *absa*1;
>   **for** *i* **to** **upb** *a*1 **do** *absa*1[*i*] := **abs** *a*1[*i*];
>   *absa*1 **end**

With a suitable declaration of priority, this extends the definition of **abs** to apply to one-dimensional arrays. Note the use of the pre-existing definition of **abs** for **real** values.

Array constants

When array assignments and operations are allowed in a language, it is convenient to be able to write explicit arrays. This can be done in APL and ALGOL 68. For example, suppose that in ALGOL 68 we have declared [1:4] **real** *a, b, c*; and also that the operator + has been defined to give the element-by-element sum of two vectors. Then the following are legal assignments:

> *a* := (3.1, 4.2, 7.4, 104.7);
> *b* := *c* + (1.1, 2.2, 3.3, 4.4);

ALGOL 68 calls this construction a "row display": it extends to arrays of higher rank, e.g. ((1, 2, 3),(4, 5, 6)) is a 2-by-3 array constant. In APL a one-dimensional array constant is just a list of the elements, e.g.

> A ← 1 2 3 4

Multi-dimensional array constants are not permitted, but there is a "re-shaping" operator to give the same effect: the 2-by-3 array given above in ALGOL 68 would be expressed in APL as

> 2 3 ρ 1 2 3 4 5 6

The left-hand operand is an array constant giving the dimensions of the array to be constructed, and the right-hand operand is an array constant listing the elements in "row-order".

Arrays in functions and subroutines

Arrays can be passed as parameters to functions and routines in most languages, though as we have already noted, few languages allow a function to return an array as a value. The function definition usually has to include a specification of the shape of an array parameter, though the actual size may be passed as a parameter itself. For example, in FORTRAN

    SUBROUTINE EXAMPLE (A, N, M)
    DIMENSION A(N, M)

In fact, in FORTRAN the array actually passed need not be the same rank as the array specified in the declarations at the head of the subroutine. This is because FORTRAN actually passes *only* the address of the start of the array.

In ALGOL 68, if a parameter is specified as **real**, a copy of the array will be passed to the routine, as it will in ALGOL 60 if an array appears as a **value** parameter. If however the parameter is specified as a **ref [ ] real** then only the reference will be passed, and as in FORTRAN the procedure will operate on the original array.

When writing general-purpose functions it is cumbersome to have to include the array sizes as parameters. PL/I provides functions LBOUND and HBOUND to allow a program to find out the size of an array. ALGOL 68 achieves the same result by a syntactic device, **lwb** and **upb**. (See below for examples.)

APL array operations

APL provides a comprehensive set of array operations, some of which have already been introduced. Since APL deals so comprehensively with arrays, it is instructive to survey its array operations briefly, and then to see to what extent they could be provided in other languages.

As already noted, the scalar operators are automatically extended to operate element-by-element on arrays. An alternative way in which scalar operators are extended to arrays is by the outer product mechanism. If A, B are arrays and f is a scalar operator, the outer product of A and B with respect to f, (written $\circ \cdot f$) consists of the result of applying f to all possible pairs of elements taken from A and B. Thus if A is the vector 1 2 3 4 5, then $A \circ . \times A$ generates a multiplication table, thus

1	2	3	4	5
2	4	6	8	10
3	6	9	12	15
4	8	12	16	20
5	10	15	20	25

A further way in which scalar operators can be applied to arrays is by the inner product mechanism, which is a generalisation of the matrix product. If A is an $m \times n$ array and B is an $n \times p$ array, the normal matrix product is defined by

$$c_{ij} = a_{i1} \times b_{ij} + a_{i2} \times b_{2j} + \ldots + a_{1n} \times b_{nj}$$

for $1 \leqslant i \leqslant m, \; 1 \leqslant j \leqslant p$

The APL inner product allows the + and $\times$ to be replaced by any scalar operators, and is generalised to operate on arrays of any number of dimensions, the product being taken over the last dimension of the first array and the first dimension of the second array (which must of course conform).

In addition to these extensions of scalar operators, there are a number of special array operations. Particularly significant are the following.

Reduction

This applies to a vector or one dimension of an array. Thus if A is a vector,

+/A gives the sum of the elements
$\times$/A gives the product of the elements
$\lceil$/A gives the largest element
etc.

If B is a two-dimensional array,

+/[1]B   gives the column sums
+/[2]B   gives the row sums.

It will be seen that the result has rank one less than the rank of the argument, hence the name.

Compression

Let A, B be vectors of n elements and let B consist only of zeros and ones. Then B/A is a vector consisting of those elements of A corresponding to the ones in B.

Thus if   A = 1   7   5   3   9
                A $\geqslant$ 5 = 0   1   1   0   1
and   (A $\geqslant$ 5)/A $-$ 7   5   9

(This selection operation provides APL with an elegant conditional jump.)

Index

B ι A gives the index in B of A, i.e. it is the inverse of the subscripting operation. If A is a vector, the result will be a vector. Thus

$$\text{'ABCDEFC'}_\iota \text{ 'CAD'} = 3 \quad 1 \quad 4$$

Ravel

If A is an array of any shape, (,A) is a vector consisting of the elements of A in row order.

Dimension

If A is an array, ρA is a vector giving the dimensions of A (i.e. the maximum value of each index – the indices start at 1). Thus

> $\rho\rho$A gives the rank of A,
> $\times/\rho$A gives the total number of elements in A, etc.

There is also an extensive range of operators for rotation, transposition, etc.

All the above operations are built into the APL system, thus making array operations elegant and powerful. Need they be built-in, or could we provide procedures in another language to do the same? We have already noted that in ALGOL 68 we can define operators over arrays. Can we define a procedure analogous to reduction?

To define such procedures we need the ability to pass scalar operators as parameters to the procedure. We can do this in POP-2: for example **nonop+** is an identifier for the addition operator. In ALGOL 60 we would need to be devious, defining, for example,

> **real procedure** *plus* (x,y); **value** x, y;
> **real** x, y ;
> *plus* := $x + y$;

and passing 'plus' as the argument. We can then define vector reduction, for example, for vectors of known size. In ALGOL 60 we would write

> **real procedure** *reduce* (*vector, n, op*);
> **value** n; **real array** *vector*; **integer** n;
> **real procedure** *op*;
> **begin real** *result*; **integer** i; *result* := *vector*[1];
>   **for** i := 2 **step** 1 **until** n **do**
>   *result* := *op*(*result, vector*[i]);
> *reduce* := *result*;
> **end**

Then if A has been declared as **real array** A[$1:p$], the APL expression +/A would become *reduce(A, p, plus)*. (The function *plus* was defined earlier.) It is an irritating feature that we must provide the size of the vector via the parameter *p*. In ALGOL 68 we could avoid this by using the operator **upb** to give the upper bound of the subscript of the vector. The definition would be

proc *reduce* = ([ ] **real** *vector, proc* (**real, real**)*op*) **real**:
begin
    real *result* := *vector*[1] ;
    for *i* **from** 2 **to upb** *vector* **do**
    result := *op* (*result, vector*[*i*]);
    result
end

Can we extend this to arrays of higher dimension? At first sight it seems so, since in ALGOL 68 we can write *n* **upb** A to get the upper bound of the *n*'th dimension of any array A. But we foul up over the fact that in the declaration of reduce we must specify the dimensionality of the array parameter. Thus we cannot define 'reduce' to work on arbitrary arrays. There is to my knowledge no language which provides the equivalent of the APL ρ operator, i.e. the ability to discover dynamically the dimensionality of an arbitrary array.

An abstract model of arrays

With the introduction of arrays we need to extend the name-reference-value concept that was introduced in Chapter 3. Let us for the moment restrict attention to one-dimensional arrays. The value of an array is in some loose sense the collection of values of its elements. We bring more precision into the definition by introducing the idea of a *descriptor*. This comprises the upper and lower index bounds, the mode of the elements (and hence by implication the amount of storage occupied by each element), and a pointer to a row of elements in a contiguous area of store. Thus corresponding to an array declared as [1:10] **int** there will be a descriptor as follows:

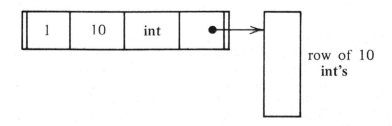

row of 10
int's

A descriptor can be associated directly with a name by an identity declaration, e.g. in ALGOL 68 notation

[   ] **int** *table* = (1, 4, 7, 10)

gives rise to

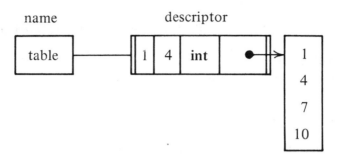

the mode of 'table' being   [   ] **int**

Alternatively, a descriptor can be associated with a reference, thus

[   ] **int** *table* := (1, 4, 7, 10)

gives rise to

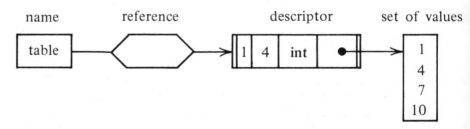

The mode of 'table' is now **ref** [   ] **int**.

We must now consider the operations of accessing and up-dating array elements. We introduce the idea of a selection operator ↓, so that $a[i]$ is a syntactically convenient notation for $a{\downarrow}(i)$. Down-arrow is a polymorphic operator: its left operand is either a descriptor or a reference to a descriptor, and its right operand is an **int** value. If the left operand is a descriptor the operator will select the appropriate value from the row, thus in this context, ↓ maps **descriptor, int** onto a value. If the left operand is a reference to a descriptor, the operator yields a reference to the selected element, i.e. ↓ maps **ref descriptor, int** onto **ref** value. If necessary, the value will then be obtained by dereferencing in the usual way. Thus if we have the declarations

$[1:10]$ **real** a; **real** b; **ref real** $a3$;

and we write

$b := a[3]$

then since b has mode **ref real** the right-hand side must yield
a **real** value. The subscripting operator yields a **ref real** value,
which is dereferenced. But if we write

$a3 := a[3]$

then the right-hand side must yield a value of mode **ref real**,
so that the reference yielded by the subscripting operation will
be assigned. This may seem excessively complex, but it ensures
that if we also declare [ ] **int** c = (1, 2, 3, 4), the assignment
$b := c[3]$ will work as expected, but we shall not be able to
change c by an assignment like $c[3] := b$, since the name c is
not associated with a reference to a descriptor, so that subscripting c will always yield an **int** value.

So far we have dealt only with one-dimensional arrays. To
extend to higher dimensions we have only to allow a descriptor
to point to a row of descriptors, thus

$[1:10, 1:5]$ **real** A

gives rise to

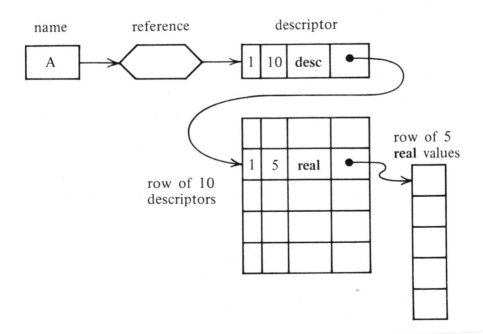

The construction $A[i,j]$ is now treated as a shorthand for $A[i][j]$ which is in turn short for $A{\downarrow}i{\downarrow}j$. This has to be parsed as $(A{\downarrow}i){\downarrow}j$ and the operation is a natural extension of the one-dimensional case. If the left operand of the first occurrence of ${\downarrow}$ is a reference to a descriptor, then it yields a reference to a value in the row – in this case a reference to another descriptor, so the second occurrence of ${\downarrow}$ will yield a reference to a value.

One further point to make is that if A, B are arrays of the same size and shape, then the assignment A:=B makes A an element-by-element *copy* of B: this copying is invoked when the polymorphic assignment operator finds the mode **ref descriptor** on the left and a **descriptor** on the right. Another way of saying this is that copying a descriptor always causes copying of the values pointed to (unlike copying a reference, which may or may not cause copying of the associated value). A further implication of this rule is that if a function has an array parameter called by value, the call will cause copying of the descriptor and hence of the array.

Array slices are also accommodated in the model. Again, we have an implied "slicing" operator, say $//$, so that $a[2{:}5]$ is a syntactic abbreviation for $a//(2,5)$. The slicing operator constructs a new descriptor and then causes the appropriate set of values to be copied.

APL extends this concept by allowing the subscript of an array itself to be an array. The extension of the formal model is straightforward, though the practical implementation leads to difficulties.

Structures

A structure is an aggregate of values whose components are identified by names. (It is essentially something that resides in store, whereas a file, which is also made up of elements identified by name, resides on disc or tape.) Data structuring facilities are a relatively new development in languages (except COBOL), and the ways in which they are provided are varied. In trying to categorise the facilities provided we can usefully ask the following questions:

(1) What elementary items can be included in a structure?
(2) Can a structure include arrays of elementary items, and can we have arrays of structures?
(3) How do we identify and refer to sub-structures and elementary items?
(4) Can we define functions of structures, and can a function have a structure as its value?

(5) Can we attach a name to a 'template' and generate multiple instances of a structure at run-time?

(6) Can we dynamically build up complicated (and introverted) structures, e.g. lists and rings?

Identifying items in data structures

A large class of structures can be regarded as trees. Typically the structure consists of a set of items which are either elementary items or substructures. The names attached to the items and substructures label the nodes of the tree. It is quite likely that these names will not be unique. Consider the example shown below.

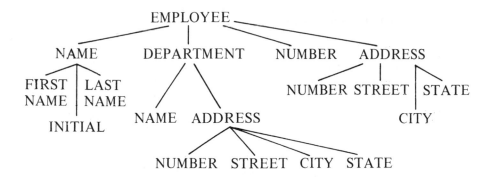

'Name' appears as the name of a subtree and as an elementary item; 'Number', 'Street' etc. occur more than once. Thus to identify an item uniquely we need to give not only its name but the path from the root of the tree. This can obviously be done 'bottom up' or 'top down', thus:

Bottom up
street IN *address* IN *department* IN *employee*   (COBOL)
name **of** *department* **of** *employee*   (ALGOL 68)

Top down
employee. department. address. street.   (PL/I)

The bottom-up approach can be regarded as focussing attention on the elementary item, whilst the top-down approach attaches more importance to the structure as a whole. Thus we might argue that the PL/I designers took a broader view than the COBOL designers, but that is probably ascribing a wholly unwarranted significance to an accident of history. In PL/I an identifier like

employee. department. street. name

is called a "fully-qualified name". If arrays of substructures or

101

elementary items are permitted, subscripts can be included as
appropriate. In some languages (COBOL, PL/I) it is not necessary always to give a fully qualified name provided that sufficient nodes are specified to make the definition unique. Thus
for the tree given above,

> street IN *department* IN *employee*

is a well-formed COBOL identifier.

The naming conventions so far introduced are syntactic
devices to identify elements of a structure. Formally we could
regard the name associated with a node as the name of a
function that will select or update that node. The 'street'
example would be written in functional notation

> street *(address(department(employee)))*.

Thus the ALGOL 68 "x **of**" and the COBOL "x IN" can
be regarded as a special syntax for a selection operation.

In ALGOL W this bracketed form is used (though this is a
syntactic device: the component selectors are not true functions). It is instructive to observe that in POP-2 the component
selectors are true functions, and that whilst we can write in
POP-2

> street *(address(department(employee)))*

the same expression can be written (still in POP-2) in postfix
form as

> *employee. department. address. street*

which corresponds exactly to the PL/I fully qualified name.

Arrays in structures

In COBOL arrays of elementary items are allowed. PL/I and
ALGOL 68 allow arrays of structures, both at the top level
and as sub-structures. Thus we can construct something of the
form

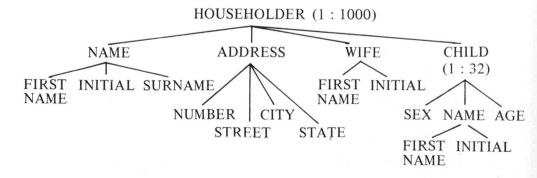

A typical reference might then be

HOUSEHOLDER(I). CHILD(J). AGE

Since 'child' is a unique identifier in this example we might write this as

CHILD(I,J). AGE

This now resembles an array element. If we have a structure

A (1 : 1000)

B   etc

where B is a simple item, we might refer to A(I). B or A.B(I) or B(I) for short. B(I) looks like an array reference, though it really means "the B in structure I". In PL/I the aggregate of B's can be regarded as an array: we call it a "non-connected" array. The movement or "factoring" of subscripts is a general property of PL/I structures.

Declaring structures

The simplest way of introducing a structure is to declare a particular variable as a structure, and to give the specification of the structure there and then. We have to describe a tree: PL/I and COBOL do this by the use of "level numbers" which are self-explanatory. The following example is in PL/I.

```
DECLARE  01  EMPLOYEE
         02  NAME
             03  FIRSTNAME
             03  INITIAL
             03  LASTNAME
         02  DEPARTMENT
             03  NAME
             03  ADDRESS
                 04  NUMBER
                 04  STREET
                 04  CITY
                 04  STATE
         02  NUMBER
         02  ADDRESS
             03  NUMBER
             03  STREET
             03  CITY
             03  STATE
```

To complete the declaration the attributes of the elementary items must be included at the appropriate point, e.g. 04 STREET CHAR(20). To make an array of such structures we would simply start the declaration

DECLARE 01 EMPLOYEE (1:1000)

This type of structure is particularly appropriate to commercial data processing. For interest, note that exactly the same structure can be declared in ALGOL 68: the form of declaration is

struct (*description of tree*) *employee*;
or   [1:1000] **struct** (----) *employee*;

The complete definition is quite long:

struct (**struct** ([1:10] **char** *firstname,*
                    char *initial,*
            [1:10] **char** *lastname*) *name,*
        struct ([1:10] **char** *name,*
            struct (**int** *number,*
                    [1:20] **char** *street,*
                    [1:10] **char** *city,*
                    [1:10] **char** *state*) *address*) *department,*
        int *number*;
        struct (**int** *number,*
                    [1:20] **char** *street,*
                    [1:10] **char** *city,*
                    [1:10] **char** *state*) *address*) *employee*;

We note that part of the length of this example arises from the duplication of the definition of an address. ALGOL 68 allows us to attach a name to a commonly occurring structure to create a template.

Thus we could write

mode *postal address* =
        struct ([1:20] **char** *street,*
                    [1:10] **char** *city,*
                    [1:10] **char** *state*);

We can now use 'postal address' in the same way as **real**; thus

postal address *address*;

makes 'address' a reference to a *new instance* of the structure defined by the mode declaration.

A similar facility is provided in ALGOL W. A *record-class* is first defined, e.g.

104

                record *employee* (**integer** *number*;
                                string (20) *name*;
                                real *pay*);

We can then create an instance of the structure by a declaration
and an assignment, e.g.

   reference (*employee*) *professor, cleaner*;
   professor := *employee*;
   cleaner := *employee*;

The declaration establishes 'professor' and 'cleaner' as *reference
variables*: their values are constrained to be pointers to records
of the class 'employee'. The assignments create two instances of
the record and assign pointers thus:

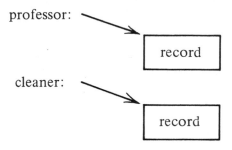

Note particularly that the assignment

   professor := *cleaner* := *employee*;

would create two pointers to the **same** record, thus:

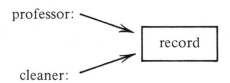

Reference variables occur in field selectors, e.g. *pay*(*professor*),
and the resulting qualified name can appear in an expression,
e.g.

   if *pay* (*professor*) < *pay* (*cleaner*) **then** ...

Reference variables can be elements of arrays, thus providing
arrays of structures; and they can appear as components of a
record. It is a feature of ALGOL W that although a record may
not contain an array as an elementary item, it may contain an
array of references to structures each of which consists of only
one item.

Structure definition in POP-2

Structures are defined in POP-2 by a system function 'recordfns'. This takes as arguments a string defining the record class, and a list giving the number of components. Its value is a set of functions; a constructor function to create a record, a destructor to decompose a record, and selector/updater functions for each component.

The facilities are illustrated in the following example, which is a transcript of an actual console session, and with the help of the comments provided should be self-explanatory if we remark that the symbol => is the "print-arrow" and causes the current contents of the stack to be printed, preceded by two asterisks.

> **vars** *newperson decomp firstname surname male;*
> *recordfns("person",[0 0 1])*
> *-> male -> surname -> firstname -> decomp -> newperson;*
> **comment** *'recordfns' is a standard function. We have used*
> *it to define a class of records (structures) called*
> *'person' each record having three components.*
> *The 0 0 1 indicates that the first two components*
> *can be items of any sort, but the third can be*
> *stored in one bit, i.e. it is a boolean. recordfns*
> *leaves on the stack five functions: a constructor*
> *to form a record, a destructor to decompose a*
> *record, and selector/updater functions for each*
> *component. These are assigned to variables by*
> *the multiple assignment;*
> **vars** *man woman;*
> *newperson(%true%) -> man; newperson(%false%) -> woman;*
> **comment** *we have used the device of 'partial application' to*
> *freeze one argument of a function. Thus man(a,b)*
> *is the same function as newperson(a, b, true) thus*
> *we avoid tedious repetition;*
> **vars** *you me she;*
> *man("david", "barron") -> me;*
> *man("lucky", "reader") -> you;*
> *woman("elizabeth", "taylor") -> she;*
> *firstname(she) =>*
> ** * elizabet*
> **comment** *=> is an operator that prints the contents of the*
> *stack. Words are truncated to 8 characters;*
> **function** *marry him her;*
> **comment** *an algorithmic form of the marriage service.*
> *the value of the function is a list expressing an*
> *appropriate sentiment. as a side-effect it updates*

> one of its arguments: it is allowed to do this
> because the arguments are structures;

if not *(male(him))* **or** *male(her)* **then** [*rather unusual*]
else *surname(him) -> surname(her);* [*lucky fellow*]
close;
end;
marry (you, me)=>
* * [*rather unusual*]
marry (you, she) =>
* * [*lucky fellow*]
firstname (she), surname(she) =>
* * *elizabet reader*

Computing with structures

The most obvious thing to do with structures, as with arrays, is to use their components as elements in the computation. Typically this is what is done in commercial data processing. When a structure element appears as the destination of an assignment, e.g.

$$employee~(i).~department~=~7;$$

we have something akin to a left-hand function. The analogy is more obvious in the notation of ALGOL W, e.g.

$$pay~(professor)~:=~pay~(professor)~+~250;$$

COBOL and PL/I allow structure assignment which copies a structure in its entirety, e.g. A = B (PL/I) or MOVE A TO B (COBOL). Obviously the structures must be the same "shape". In both languages a selective structure assignment is possible using the qualifier "BY NAME" or "CORRESPONDING". Thus A = B BY NAME (PL/I), or MOVE B TO A CORRESPONDING (COBOL) will assign only those components of A that have the same names as components of B.

Comparison and copying of structures

Once elaborate computing with structures is permitted, we need to take great care over definitions. For example, in POP-2, if the value of a variable A is a structure, there is associated with A a pointer to the structure. Then the assignment A → B creates another pointer to the *same* structure. The comparison A = B only gives the result **true** if A, B are identical pointers. Even though a structure C may be an identical copy of another structure D, the predicate C = D will be **false**, because the variables are pointing to two separate structures. To test for equality in the general sense we need a recursive function to compare structures element-by-element. (Recursive because any element of a structure may itself be a structure.) POP-2 has a system function 'copy', thus copy(A) → B makes B a copy of A at the top level: to create an absolute copy it is again necessary to use a recursive function.

A similar situation is found in ALGOL 68. Since both operands of a comparison are dereferenced, it is impossible to use the "=" operation to compare two references for equality. To get round this difficulty a new operator IS is introduced (with the obvious converse ISNT). Thus

> a IS b

is true if a, b are identical references, whereas $a = b$ is true if a, b are references to identical objects.

Dynamic structures

To deal with dynamic structures it is necessary that the language should allow manipulation of references (or pointers). To illustrate this we consider the manipulation of a binary tree in ALGOL 68 and in PL/I. The simple binary tree

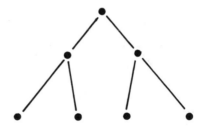

is made up of nodes, each of which comprises a data item (which without loss of generality we can assume to be an integer), a left branch and a right branch, these last two being pointers to further nodes, or special markers in the case of a leaf. Pictorially, we can represent the node as a box with three compartments:

integer
left branch
right branch

In ALGOL 68 we would first define a new data type, which we call a cell, thus:

108

mode *cell* = **struct** (**int** *item*, **ref cell** *lb*, **ref cell** *rb*);

This defines a cell as a structure of three components: the first is an integer and the other two are references to cells (note the recursive nature of the definition). Having defined a new mode we can use it like any other (e.g. **real**) thus the declaration

    cell *p, q, r, s,*

creates four instances of this new kind of object, and associates the names *p, q, r, s* with references to them thus:

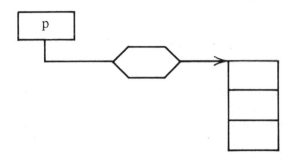

We can now fill the fields of the cell by collateral assignment, thus

    p := (12, *q, r*)

creates the structure

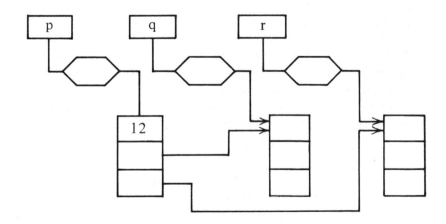

This has left the left and right branches of *q* and *r* "dangling", and they are best plugged by the special quantity "nil". Thus if we write

    cell *p, q, r*;
    p := (12, *q, r*); *q* := (8, *nil, nil*); *r* := (16, *nil, nil*);

we will have set up the tree

If we want now to add a further node with value 14 as the left branch of the node 16, we would have to amend the original declaration to **cell** *p, q, r, s* and add the statements

$$s := (14, nil, nil); lb \text{ of } r := s;$$

This is cumbersome and unsatisfactory, and it is easy to see that the trouble arises because every cell has to have a name. If we are to get anywhere we must be able to have anonymous structures, just as we can have anonymous scalar values in expressions. The mechanism is there: we recall that **real** *x* is an abbreviation for **ref real** *x* = **loc real**; so **cell** *p* is an abbreviation for **ref cell** *p* = **loc cell**, where **loc cell** is a local generator that acquires storage for a variable of mode **cell**. However, there is no need to use a generator in a declaration: it can be used anywhere that we want to introduce a cell. Thus the tree that we constructed above using variables *p, q, r* could be extended without introducing a new name, thus:

$$lb \text{ of } r := \textbf{loc cell} := (14, nil, nil);$$

In fact, we need one further refinement to make this a useful system. All the cells so far created have been local, so that the space will be lost at the end of the block in which they were declared or created. This is unlikely to be helpful, and in practice we would use **heap** generators, since heap storage is subject to a garbage collection mechanism, and is only discarded when there are no references by which it can be accessed. We would therefore create the tree as follows.

> **ref cell** *p* = **heap cell**; c *the root of the tree needs a name* c
> *item* **of** *p* := 12; *lb* **of** *p* := **heap cell** := (8, *nil, nil*);
>   *rb* **of** *p* := **heap cell** := (16, *nil, nil*);
>   *lb* **of** *rb* **of** *p* := **heap cell** := (14, *nil, nil*);

An alternative way of adding the last node that would probably be more use in practice would be to write

> **ref cell** *ptr* := *rb* **of** *p*;
> *lb* **of** *ptr* := **heap cell** := (14, *nil, nil*);

Here *ptr* is a local variable, but since its use is purely temporary that is of no matter. We note in passing that **heap** storage is also used whenever an array is declared with **flex** bounds, e.g. a **string**. The existence of this kind of storage management is an essential prerequisite for the convenient manipulation of dynamic structures.

Dynamic structures in PL/I

Having made this assertion, we now turn to PL/I, which does not provide such a garbage collection facility. It has a generator facility which yields anonymous storage areas (to be accessed by pointers), but relies on the programmer to de-allocate storage which is no longer required. This is, of course, a great inconvenience and a fruitful source of errors. The language allows dynamic structures to be grouped into "areas", so that an entire group can be de-allocated by a single statement, but this is at most a palliative and does not really solve the problem.

Dynamic structures are achieved in PL/I using two categories of storage – CONTROLLED and BASED. We have already met CONTROLLED storage: if a variable is declared with this attribute then no storage is reserved until an explicit ALLO-CATE command is issued, and once created the reference exists until cancelled by an explicit FREE command. It is worth noting that the sequence

        DCL A CONTROLLED
        . . . .

        . . . .
        ALLOCATE A

        . . . .
        ALLOCATE A

will generate two incarnations of the variable A, of which only the most recently produced is accessible by use of the name A. In other words, this is a form of stack storage, where the stack is pushed by ALLOCATE and popped by FREE.

BASED storage is a variant of CONTROLLED storage, in which the declaration specifies also a POINTER that will contain the "address" of the variable (which may be a simple variable, an array or a structure). Thus a pointer has much in common with a **ref** variable in ALGOL 68. However, since there are no consistency checks it is a much more dangerous beast.

Suppose we have the declarations

        DCL P POINTER;
        DCL X . . . BASED(P);

No storage is reserved for the variable X until we obey an

ALLOCATE(X) statement. At this stage storage is found and the reference to this storage is assigned as the value of P. Thereafter, an occurrence of X will be regarded as standing for the reference that is the value of P: X is said to be implicitly qualified. The pointer can be made explicit, e.g.

```
DCL (P, Q) POINTER;
DCL X . . . BASED(P);
. . .
ALLOCATE(X) SET(Q);
```

will cause the reference to the storage created for X to be assigned as the value of Q, i.e. Q "points to" X. Subsequently, the notation Q → X is used to signify "X pointed to by Q"; the occurrence of X is now explicitly qualified. (X on its own still means "X pointed to by P"). At this stage the reader may with some justice feel that this part of PL/I shows signs of muddled thinking. ("A camel is a horse designed by a committee".) As before, successive uses of ALLOCATE without an intervening FREE generate a push-down stack of references. Alternatively, the references can be kept accessible as in the following example.

```
DCL P(100) POINTER /* AN ARRAY OF 100
      POINTERS */;
DCL X . . . BASED(P);
. . .
DO I = 1 TO 100;
. . .
ALLOCATE(X) SET(P(I));
. . .
END
```

This will fill the array P with references to successive instances of X. We shall see how this facility can be exploited when we consider input/output in Chapter 7.

We now sketch the PL/I approach to setting up a binary tree structure. We first make some declarations:

```
DCL (P, Q, R, PTR) POINTER;
DCL 1 CELL BASED(PTR),
      2 ITEM FIXED . . .
      2 LB POINTER,
      2 RB POINTER;
```

Here CELL is defined as a structure with three components, two of which are POINTERS. Since it is declared with the attribute BASED, it can be replicated by successive occurrences of ALLOCATE. (Compare an ALGOL 68 **mode** declaration and

112

its subsequent use in a generator.) Thus

        ALLOCATE(CELL) SET(P);
        ALLOCATE(CELL) SET(Q);
        ALLOCATE(CELL) SET(R);

will create three CELLs pointed to by P, Q and R.
    If we now wish to create a simple node thus:

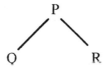

we can fill in the fields of the cell pointed to by P as follows:

        P → CELL. ITEM   = 3;
        P → CELL. LB   = Q;
        P → CELL. RB   = R;

If at the start of the program we put the sequence

        ALLOCATE(CELL) SET(NEWCELL);
        NEWCELL → CELL. ITEM   = 0;
        NEWCELL → CELL. LB   = NULL;
        NEWCELL → CELL. RB   = NULL;

we shall construct a cell representing a terminal node. Then

        ALLOCATE(CELL) SET(Q);
        Q → CELL = NEWCELL → CELL;

elsewhere in the program will create a copy of this terminal node pointed to by Q. It should now be apparent how PL/I would go about the problem of setting up a complete binary tree: it should also be apparent that the process is set about with pitfalls for the unwary, and like matrimony should only be undertaken "...reverently, discreetly, advisedly, soberly...".

6

STRINGS

The Chief Defect of Henry King
   Was chewing little bits of String.
At last he swallowed some which tied
   Itself in ugly Knots inside.
             Belloc: *Cautionary Tales for Children*

It used to be said that "scientific" programming languages could be characterised by the fact that they provided little if any capability for character string manipulation. This facile distinction is no longer true, since languages like PL/I and ALGOL 68 provide extensive character manipulation. However, it was certainly a valid criticism of FORTRAN and ALGOL 60.

Characters in FORTRAN are an obvious after-thought. The Standard says that we can store characters in any type of variable (though the number of characters packed in each variable will depend on the implementation). It prescribes ways of reading and printing such strings (A-format) and specifies that Hollerith strings can appear as arguments of CALLed sub-routines (but not, for some mysterious reason, as arguments of functions). Apart from reading and immediately printing them, there is not much you can safely do with characters in FORTRAN. If they are stored in REAL variables, you cannot even move them with safety, since on many machines the simple assignment A = B will cause the supposed floating-point number in B to be standardised, with disastrous results in the character representation. You cannot test character strings for equality: to avoid standardisation you have to use INTEGER variables, and the subtraction invoked by IF(I.EQ.J) is likely to cause arithmetic overflow, if one of the packed character strings appears to be a negative integer. (The rule that A-format input is space-filled *from the right* more or less guarantees trouble.)

The designers of ALGOL 60 did not fall into this trap. They allow a data type **string** as a procedure parameter, but provide neither a way of declaring a string variable nor any operations upon strings. The only use of a **string** variable in ALGOL 60 is as a parameter of a procedure with a code (i.e. machine-code or assembler) body. Since such a procedure cannot yield a **string** value its usefulness is minimal.

Before considering how other languages order things better,

114

it is worth making an important observation. Operations on strings can be divided into two categories. In the first place there are operations such as comparison and moving of strings (as for example in an alphabetic sort). In the second class comes decomposition of strings into substrings, selective replacement of substrings, construction of new strings by concatenation, etc. The characteristic feature of operations of the first type is that strings remain of the same length, whereas the operations of the second class produce strings of variable (and unpredictable) length. To deal with these satisfactorily requires a dynamic storage allocation facility, and this may explain why such facilities are so rare in languages.

COBOL strings

COBOL does not have dynamic storage, and so can only manipulate fixed-length strings. In a sense, COBOL manipulates only strings, since all the elementary items within a file are declared as character strings. (Unfortunately, character-oriented machines went out as COBOL came in, which is probably why qualifier "USAGE IS COMPUTATIONAL" was introduced, to indicate those strings that should be given a different internal representation.) In a COBOL file definition, character strings are defined by a pro-forma or PICTURE. Thus

08 COST PICTURE IS 9999

specifies COST to be a 4-digit integer. In a picture, 9 signifies a decimal digit, A an alphabetic character, B a blank and X an alphanumeric, thus the picture of a typical post-code is AA9B9AA. We see that the picture specifies the length of the character string and may restrict the kind of character that can occur in a particular position. (Pictures also indicate other attributes of a variable, thus S prefixed to a numeric item indicates that it is signed, and V within a numeric item indicates the assumed position of the decimal point. Note that S99V9 specifies a *three-character* item: the S and the V simply give information about the arithmetic to be used.)

The simplest string operation in COBOL is assignment – MOVE A TO B. Strings can be compared and ordered, e.g.

      IF NAME EQUAL "SMITH" THEN ....
or   IF NAME-1 GREATER THAN NAME-2 THEN ....

The category of a string can also be determined, e.g.

      IF NAME IS ALPHABETIC ......

will be true if and only if NAME is composed entirely of

alphabetic characters.

An interesting form of string manipulation in COBOL is the implicit manipulation caused by the use of "editing characters" in pictures. This is used to prepare material for output. (In COBOL it is necessary to generate in core an exact image of the printed line – see Chapter 7 for more discussion of this point.)

If a variable is defined with a picture that includes editing characters, then whenever a value is assigned to it the value will be edited accordingly. For example, suppose we have declarations

    N1 PICTURE IS S99V99
    N2 PICTURE IS +Z9.99
    N3 PICTURE IS -Z9.99
    N4 PICTURE IS £*9.99CR

N1 is a 4-digit signed number with two digits after the decimal point. Suppose its value is 08.74. Then

    MOVE N1 TO N2 will set N2 to +b8.74 (b indicates blank)
    MOVE N1 TO N3 will set N3 to bb8.74
    MOVE N1 TO N4 will set N4 to £*8.74CR

The explanation of this is that +, –, Z, £, * and CR are some of the "editing symbols" available in COBOL: + signifies an explicit sign, – signifies a minus sign if negative and a blank if positive, Z indicates a zero-suppressed digit, * stands for a "cheque-protect" digit (replace zero by *), £ and point stand for themselves, and CR is a banker's plus sign. The COBOL editing system, though ingenious, is full of pitfalls: the most obvious one is to

    MOVE Q1 TO Q2

where Q1 has picture 99V9 and Q2 has picture 9.99 (i.e. the actual decimal point does not correspond to the assumed point).

More elaborate string manipulation in COBOL is provided by the EXAMINE verb. This is a portmanteau verb that allows the user to scan a value, counting and/or replacing occurrences of a specified character. Its options are shown in the diagram. (Note that "tallying" is a synonym for "counting".)

The count is kept in a variable TALLY whose name is a reserved word. Examples of the use of EXAMINE are:

    EXAMINE AMOUNT REPLACING LEADING ZEROES BY "*"
    EXAMINE SPLOD TALLYING UNTIL FIRST ","
    EXAMINE PLOD TALLYING ALL SPACES REPLACING BY
        "/"

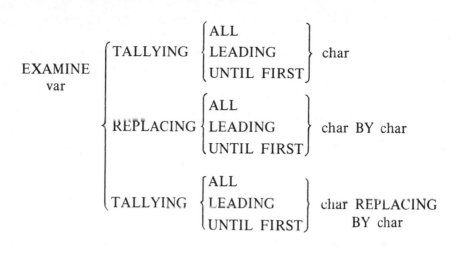

Strings in PL/I

PL/I attempts to provide some facilities for manipulating substrings without going in for full dynamic storage. Three forms of declaration are permitted.

      DCL STR1 CHAR(20)

declares STR1 as a fixed-length string of 20 characters. When an assignment is made to STR1 the value will be space-filled if it is too short and truncated if it is too long.

      DCL STR2 CHAR(20) VARYING

declares STR2 to be a string of varying length, not exceeding 20 characters (thus space will be reserved for 20 characters). The main use of VARYING is to ensure that when two strings are concatenated the trailing blanks of the first string will be discarded. (A VARYING string is presumed to finish at the rightmost non-blank character.)

    The third form of declaration resembles the COBOL method: it is provided because it allows restrictions to be placed on the characters that can appear in a string, by providing a pro-forma or PICTURE. This is made up of the characters A, X and 9: A signifies an alphabetic character or blank, X indicates a position that can hold any character, and 9 indicates a position that must contain a decimal digit or a blank. Thus

      DCL S PIC 'XXXXX'
 and DCL S CHAR(5)

are equivalent declarations, but

      DCL T PIC 'A9999'

restricts T to a five-character string in which the first character is alphabetic and the next four are numeric.

Once declared, string variables can be used in any sensible context, e.g. IF STR1 = 'IBM' THEN .... Strings can appear in comparisons, e.g. IF STR1 < STR2 THEN ... but care is needed because the result of such a comparison may be dependent on the collating sequence built into the internal character code of the particular computer in use. It is usually safe to assume that the sequence is such that the letters of the alphabet are in ascending order, so that, for example, F < Q is **true**, but comparison of non-alphabetic strings is dangerous. If strings of different lengths are compared, the shorter string is effectively padded with blanks in the comparison.

The only operator in PL/I that takes string arguments is the concatenation operator, ‖. Thus if we have

```
DCL ST1, ST2 CHAR(10) VARYING
ST1 = "GOOD"
ST2 = "GRIEF"
```

then the expression ST1‖" "‖ST2 has the value "GOOD GRIEF".

Although this is the only string-handling operator, further string-handling facilities are provided in PL/I by the built-in functions SUBSTR, LENGTH, INDEX, VERIFY and TRANS-LATE.

The value of SUBSTR(ST, N, M) is the string of M characters starting at character position N in the string ST. If M is omitted the substring is assumed to extend to the end of the parent string. SUBSTR can also be used on the left-hand side of an assignment (cf. chapter 4) as for example

```
IF SUBSTR (ST, 6, 3) = "CAT" THEN
   SUBSTR (ST, 6, 3) = "DOG";
```

The value of LENGTH(S) is a count of the number of charac-ters in the string S – often useful in a subroutine that has a string variable as a parameter. The function INDEX(S1, S2) takes two string arguments: if S2 is a substring of S1 the value of the INDEX function is the character position within S1 at which S2 starts. If S2 is not a substring of S1, the value is zero. Thus if S1, S2 have been declared with the VARYING attribute, we can remove S2 from S1 as follows:

```
N = INDEX(S1, S2);
IF N ¬= 0 THEN
S1 = SUBSTR(S1, 1, N–1)‖SUBSTR(S1, N+LENGTH
     (S1)–LENGTH(S2)–N+1);
```

The value of VERIFY(S1, S2) is zero if every character of S1 appears somewhere in S2: if there is a character that is in S1 but not in S2 the value of the function is the position of that character (or the first such character). Thus

IF VERIFY(S, '0123456789') = 0 THEN ...

is the PL/I equivalent of the COBOL construction IF S IS NUMERIC THEN ..,. The function TRANSLATE allows systematic substitution within a string. Thus the value of TRANSLATE(S1, S2, S3) is a string constructed from S1 as follows. S1 is scanned from left to right, and any occurrence of a character included in *S3* is replaced by the correponding character from *S2*. (This confusing definition needs to be read several times.) Thus the effect of the statement S = TRANS-LATE(S, '*' ' ') is to replace all the blanks in S by asterisks.

ALGOL 68 strings

ALGOL 68 provides quite powerful string handling facilities as a by-product of its array-handling facilities (see Chapter 5). There is a basic mode **char**, which as its name implies signifies a value that is a single character. The actual value stored will depend on the character code of the computer, but if *c* is a variable of mode **char**, **abs** *c* yields a unique integer which is the integer value of the internal binary code for the particular character. Conversely, **repr** *i* where *i* has a value of mode **int** performs the inverse translation.

In ALGOL 68 a string is just an array of characters: formally the mode **string** is defined by

mode *string* = **flex** [1:0] **char**;

i.e. an array with dynamic bounds that will automatically expand and contract to accommodate the strings assigned to it. This involves dynamic store allocation and garbage collection that can add 10% or 20% to the run-time of the program. For fixed length strings the programmer can define his own mode, e.g.

mode *string* 10 = [1 : 10] **char**;

Substrings are just segments of an array, thus if we declare

string *S*1;

then *S*1 [1] is the first character of the string, *S*1 [**upb** *S*1] is the last character, *S*1 [1 : 3] is the string comprising the first three characters of *S*1, and so on. It is tempting to try to attach a name to the substring in the following manner:

mode *string* 3 = [1 : 3] **char**;

ref string 3 *ss*; **string** $S1$;
$S1$:= ....
ss := $S1$ [(**upb** $S1$ – 3) : **upb** $S1$]

to make *ss* a reference to the string made up of the last 3 characters of $S1$. However, this is not allowed: a slice of a flexible array creates a transient reference, which cannot be assigned. (This is because the bounds of the array that was sliced may later change in such a way that the slice no longer exists.)

Literal strings are permitted, e.g.

string *s*; *s* := "*a.string.denotation*";

Note the use of '.' to indicate blanks in a string. Operators taking strings are provided: concatenation (denoted by '+') and the full range of comparisons. As we have noted, the component characters of a string can be accessed by indexing. If the indexing capability is not needed, it is often more efficient to use the mode **bytes**. This denotes a value that is a fixed-length character string, the length being such that it will fit exactly into one machine word. (Exactly what this length is can be ascertained by using the function *byteswidth*: this is an example of an environment enquiry that makes possible machine-independent programming in ALGOL 68.) As with other modes, we also have **long bytes, long long bytes,** etc. for longer strings. For example, in an implementation where byteswidth = 4, we can write **long long bytes** *s* = "*a.good. book.*" to create a 12-character constant.

SNOBOL 4

To do serious text manipulation one needs much more sophisticated facilities, in particular pattern matching. These facilities can be provided by a package of procedures, or by a special purpose language. SNOBOL 4 is probably the best known and most versatile string processing language. The most fundamental operation in SNOBOL 4 is comparison of strings. A typical SNOBOL match would be

STRING "ED" : S (FOUND)

If "ED" occurs as a substring of STRING the match succeeds, and control goes to FOUND. (S stands for Success: each statement can have success and failure successors specified, with "next statement" as default.) Patterns with alternatives can be set up for subsequent use in matching by

VOWEL = 'A' 'E' 'I' 'O' 'U'

With this pattern set up, the construction

STRING VOWEL

will yield a successful match if STRING contains a vowel, and

STRING VOWEL VOWEL

will be successful if STRING contains two consecutive vowels. It is often convenient to include "don't care" characters in patterns, e.g.

STRING VOWEL LEN(3) 'F'

is successful if STRING contains a vowel and an F separated by three arbitrary characters. In such a case it is often desirable to know exactly what particular pattern satisfied the match. For example, if we write

    PAT = VOWEL LEN (3) 'F'
    NPAT = PAT.Z
    .
    .
    .
    STRING NPAT   :S(FOUND)

then if STRING contains a vowel separated from an F by three arbitrary characters, control will go to FOUND because the match succeeded, and the variable Z will be assigned as its value the string that actually matched up. The other vital feature of SNOBOL is matching with replacement.

STRING VOWEL = '*'

will replace the *leftmost* vowel in STRING by an asterisk.

LOOP STRING VOWEL = '*'   :S(LOOP)

will replace all vowels in STRING by asterisks.

Space does not permit a detailed exposition of SNOBOL4. The reader should be able to appreciate the potential of the language, and is urged to follow up the references given in Chapter 10.

Bit strings

The manipulation of bit strings is usually regarded as one activity which is incontrovertibly outside the scope of high level languages. However, despite the necessarily machine dependent effects, some bit-string manipulation is possible in a high level language and such facilities are provided in PL/I and ALGOL 68.

A bit-string variable in PL/I is declared using the attribute BIT, e.g.

DCL MASK ˙BIT(16)

and bit-string constants are allowed in programs, e.g.

MASK = 1111000011110000B.

The logical operators **not** (⌐) **and** (&) and **or** (|) are provided, and operate in parallel on all the bits in the bit string in the usual way.

The internal representation of variables can be explicitly displayed in a bit-string using the built-in function UNSPEC. Thus if we declare X as a real variable and BS as a 32 bit string

BS = UNSPEC(X)

will set BS to the bit string which is the floating-point internal representation of the value of X. UNSPEC is a pseudo-variable (left-hand function) and so allows a floating point value to be explicitly set as a bit string, e.g. UNSPEC(X) = <*bit string*>. Automatic representation conversions are made where appropriate. Thus if we declare

```
DCL   BS BIT (32)
      CS CHAR (32)
      I   FIXED
      X   REAL
```

then:

   (i)   CS = BS
         will generate a character string of '1' and '0' characters,
  (ii)   BS = CS
         will create a bit string if CS is a string containing only '1' and '0' characters,
 (iii)   I = BS
         will convert the bit string BS, treating it as an unsigned integer,   and
 (iv)   X = BS will first convert the bit string as an unsigned integer and then convert that integer to a real. Note carefully the distinction between X = BS and UNSPEC(X) = BS.

In ALGOL 68 we can declare a **bits** variable, e.g. **bits** *bs*; or a two-word bits variable by **long bits** *bbs*; and so on. The environment enquiry

    i := *bits width*;

will give the number of bits per word. In the same way that a **bytes** value is a word of **chars**, so a **bits** value is a word of **bools**, and the usual logical operations can be applied in parallel to all the bits in a word. There is a selector function: i **elem** bs selects the ith bit in bs. There is also a shifting operator, which is likely to be highly implementation dependent.

7

INPUT–OUTPUT

Free from all meaning, whether good or bad,
And in one word, heroically mad.
Dryden: *Absalom and Achitophel*

Introduction

Input–output is generally found to be one of the least satisfactory aspects of any language, possibly because it is the one
area where the designer cannot entirely ignore the outside
world. In the early days of high level languages the compiler
had to generate the whole of the input–output control, so that
the idiosyncrasies of the hardware were reflected directly into
the language. Nowadays the physical input–output system is
usually concealed in decent obscurity by the operating system:
this makes it possible to provide a cleaner I/O system within
the high level language at the expense of pushing the complication of dealing with real devices into the even less satisfactory
realm of the job control language.

   In this chapter we shall attempt to establish a semi-abstract
model of the input/output process that is applicable to most
languages, illustrating the critical points by examples from a
number of languages. Older languages tend to talk about
specific devices, but a more modern approach (which we shall
follow in our model) is to see the program communicating with
an environment that consists of a number of conceptual files.
These files have names to identify them within the program,
and the correspondence between these internal names and
external files or devices is usually set up by job control statements outside the language. It may also be necessary to define
some of the physical characteristics of a file (e.g. record length,
blocking factor, access method, etc.), and this information may
be provided by special language statements, or by job control
statements outside the program (or by a combination of the
two – possibly the least satisfactory state of affairs). Files must
be opened before they can be used, and closed when they are
no longer required (though the opening and closing may not
be explicitly specified in the program). The act of opening a
file involves communication with the operating system to
ensure that the required device or external file is allocated to

the program, and possibly to set up buffers. Conversely, closing a file informs the operating system that the device is no longer required, unwinds any multiple buffering arrangement, and releases the space used for buffers.

File attributes

Each conceptual file is described by a number of attributes:

> access mode: read only (card reader, magnetic tape)
> write only (line printer, magnetic tape)
> read/write (disc)

(Note that a teleprinter is not a read/write file: it is a read-only file (keyboard) associated with a write-only file (printer).)

> file organisation: sequential (card reader, line printer,
> magnetic tape)
> non-sequential (disc)

Non-sequential files can be further subdivided according to the file organisation used (e.g. index-sequential, etc.).

This classification of files gives rise to great flexibility. For example, a card reader is regarded as a file that is read-only, sequential, with record length 80 bytes. *Any* file with these attributes will be acceptable as a "card reader", thus a program written to read cards may be fed from a tape on which input has been spooled, or from a synchronous communications line connected to a mini-computer acting as an "intelligent terminal". Indeed, a conceptual file may be just an area of storage in the core-store, used first as a write-only output file and later as a read-only input file.

The two types of I/O

There are two distinct ways in which a program can be connected to a conceptual file: this reflects the fact that I/O may involve two separate kinds of operation. There is the physical transfer of information to or from the file, and there may also be a representation conversion (e.g. from a 2-s complement binary integer to a string of decimal characters preceded by a sign). One mode of connection includes the appropriate conversion as an integral part of the connection, whereas the other mode of connection transfers information between program and file as a series of bytes without any conversion, i.e. the external and internal representations are identical. In scientific computation, "external" I/O (e.g. reading cards and printing lines) involves format conversion, whilst "backing store" transfers (which are not intended for human consumption) are made without conversion. However, in commercial data processing it is much more common for data to be transferred unconverted, any necessary formatting being carried out explicitly within the program. Nomenclature in this area is confused and confusing. Fortran describes the two types of I/O as "formatted" and "unformatted": PL/I uses the terms "list-directed" and "record directed". ALGOL 68 describes I/O with representation conversion as "character I/O", but this is misleading since a string-processing program might do all its I/O without conversion. In order to avoid unintended meanings being read into words, we shall use the neutral terms "Type 1" and "Type 2".

Type 1 Input–Output

The distinguishing feature of type 1 input–output is that there is a representation conversion associated with each transfer: the conversion rules may be implicit, or may be explicitly stated. The input or output device is regarded as a serial character file, upon which is superimposed some sort of structuring into records or lines. It is useful to distinguish between systems that use a structuring that is directly related to the hardware, and systems in which the structuring is more user-oriented. We call these hard and soft structured systems respectively.

Typical of hard structured systems is the FORTRAN I/O system. Here the properties of unit-record devices determine the structure: input is in 80-byte records and output is in 132-byte records (usually); the format of each record has to be specified, and a whole record is read or written by each I/O instruction. Soft structured systems are typified by ALGOL 68 and PL/I. On input, end of card is treated as a number terminator, but otherwise the input is just a sequence of bytes, and one input instruction reads as many cards as may be necessary to provide the values required. (Such a system will evidently adapt much more comfortably to conversational terminal I/O than a hard structured system.) For printed output, the hard structured system provides page throw and "skip-to-channel" paper motion that will depend on the printer control loop. The soft structured system regards a printer as an output file that is structured into pages made up of lines, so a typical paper movement will be "skip to line n", or "skip m lines".

The control of paper motion for printed output in a hard structured system is particularly confusing to the programmer. In FORTRAN, each WRITE statement will normally start a new line, the spacing being determined by the first character

126

of the print record (which is not itself printed). The usual convention is as follows:

blank	= print on next line
0	= leave one blank line
1	= skip to head of next page
+	= print on same line as before
any other	
character	= illegal

Woe betide the programmer who forgets this and tries to print a table in which the first character on each line is "1"! COBOL appears at first to be soft structured, since typical output lines are

WRITE PRINT-LINE FROM FINAL-LINE AFTER 2

indicating that the contents of FINAL-LINE are to be transferred to the file record PRINT-LINE, and printed after 2 blank lines. However, the programmer is still required to specify an extra character at the start of PRINT-LINE so that the system can insert a carriage control character! As an alternative, COBOL allows the construction

WRITE.........AFTER *<variable name>*

Incredibly, in this case the value of the specified variable must be one of the carriage control characters, *not* the number of lines to be left blank!

In a soft-structured system the page layout is achieved by unambiguous instructions (see below), and the complications of carriage control characters are hidden from the user. (After all, his output may be going to a teletype, which does not expect a carriage control character.)

Input–output formatting

Formatting is the term used to describe the definition of the conversions to be carried out as part of Type 1 I/O. The first choice is whether to make this implicit or explicit: in general hard-structured systems require it to be explicit, whereas soft-structured systems give the choice. FORTRAN is typical of the former: except in non-standard dialects such as WATFOR, all READ and WRITE statements must have an associated FORMAT statement. Typical "soft" systems are PL/I and ALGOL 68, which give all combinations as shown in the figure.

	Implicit Format	Explicit Format
Input	GET LIST	GET EDIT
	read	read f
Output	PUT LIST	PUT EDIT
	print	print f

(PL/I in CAPITALS, ALGOL 68 in lower case)

The arguments for and against implicit formatting are rather different depending on whether we are considering input or output. In general, it is most convenient for input to be in a "free format" form, using simple rules, e.g. "a number starts with a digit, and is terminated by a character that is not a digit or a point" (together with further rules to allow signs, to prevent a number having two decimal points, etc.). ALGOL 68 and PL/I both provide this type of free format input: in contrast, the insistence of (standard) FORTRAN on strict explicit formatting of input reflects the historical influence of punch-card accounting machines on its designers. (If you have an un-intelligent punch-card machine you have to tell it which columns of the card contain a number. A computer is sufficiently intelligent to find out for itself.)

On output, implicit formatting is attractive for program testing runs, and for beginners, but for neatly laid-out reports it is almost always necessary to use explicitly formatted output. The major disadvantage of implicitly formatted output is that the standard format chosen by the system has to be sufficiently general to cover all eventualities, for example allowing sufficient digits for the full precision of a value.

For implicitly formatted output, the page is usually regarded as being divided into a number of fields (analogous to a tab setting on a typewriter), and items are printed in successive fields across the page. Explicit page layout control has to be provided: in PL/I this is done by adding options to the PUT statement, so that the value of a variable A can be printed in an appropriate standard format in any of the following ways:

PUT LIST (A)	will print at the next tab position on the current line
PUT SKIP LIST (A)	will print at the start of a new line
PUT PAGE LIST (A)	will print at the start of the first line of the next page
PUT SKIP(n) LIST (A)	will advance n lines (i.e. leave $n-1$ empty lines) and print at the start of the line

PUT LINE(*n*) LIST (A)   will print at the start of
                          line *n* on the current page

Similar facilities are provided in ALGOL 68 by the procedures
newpage, newline, space and backspace. These take one argument of mode **file** (we shall learn more about **file** variables
later): the identifiers standin and standout denote the standard
I/O channels (cf. SYSIN and SYSOUT in IBM terminology).
The first two of these layout procedures are self explanatory;
space skips one character (normally leaving a blank space) in
the current line, and backspace moves one character back in
the current line to overprint the previous character. (Whether
the implementer can actually do this with the hardware at his
disposal is another question.) The backspace procedure will not
move back beyond the beginning of the current line, and the
sequence backspace-space will not erase a character (hence the
reservation about space leaving a blank position in the line).
A particularly ingenious and useful facility is that these layout
procedures can appear without a parameter within the argument
list of a call of the print procedure (which by definition refers
to the standard output channel, i.e. system printer). For
example,

> *print* ((*newpage,* "STATISTICS", *newline,* "*Mean* = ", *mean,*
> "*s. d.* = ", *deviation*))

As the example just given suggests, the ALGOL 68 print
procedure is particularly powerful. Its argument can include
variables and constants of any mode (including strings), and if
an array name or structure name is included in the parameter
list, all the components of the array or structure are printed.
It is also possible to include an expression as an item in the
print list.

Another interesting feature of implicitly formatted I/O in
ALGOL 68 is that the layout procedures can be used to control input, either directly, using the parameter 'standin' to
denote the system input channel, or without a parameter as an
item in the argument list of the read procedure (implicitly
specifying standin as the channel). Thus if the system input
channel is a card reader, the statement

> *read* (*newline, x, newline, y*)

will ignore the remainder of the current card, read a value for
x from the next card, ignore the remainder of that card and
read a value for *y* from the next card in sequence. This should
be compared with the call *read* (*x, y*), which will read values
for *x* and *y* starting from the current reading position and

ignoring card boundaries.

A disadvantage of implicitly formatted output is that the values are not explicitly identified on the output page. To get over this, PL/I provides a further mode of I/O – DATA directed. If we write

PUT SKIP DATA A, B, C

the printed output will take the form

A = ...   B = ...   C = ...

Conversely, if we use DATA-directed input, writing

GET DATA A, B, C,

then any of the following would be acceptable input lines:

A = 30.7   B = 20.4   C = 10.5
C = 10.5   B = 20.4   A = 30.7
A = 30.7   C = 10.5   B = 20.4
etc.

DATA directed input is probably the simplest for a non-specialist to understand: it also has the unusual feature that (provided an appropriate medium is used) output produced by the PUT DATA statement is in a form acceptable to the GET DATA statement for re-input.

A further useful facility in PL/I (which applies to DATA, EDIT and LIST directed input) is that by adding the word COPY to the input statement a copy of the input can be printed, thus

GET LIST (A, B, C) COPY

is equivalent to the group of statements

GET LIST (A)
PUT SKIP LIST (A)
GET LIST (B)
PUT SKIP LIST (B)
GET LIST (C)
PUT SKIP LIST (C)

Explicit format specification

We now turn to I/O of type 1 with explicit format specification. This can occur in both "hard" and "soft" systems. The difference is that in a hard system the format specification describes a physical record, whilst in a soft system it describes the formatting of the information being input or output by

130

the particular statement. Thus in FORTRAN we write

READ (n, m) <*data list*>

where n is a channel number and m is the label of a FORMAT statement: the FORMAT is clearly associated with the channel. In PL/I on the other hand, we write

GET EDIT (<*data list*>) (<*format list*>)

clearly associating the format list and the data list. In fact, it is possible to break up the data list and associate a format list with each part, e.g.

GET EDIT (*data list*) (*format list*) (*data list*) (*format list*);

Similarly, in ALGOL 68 we write

printf ((<*format*>, <*variable list*>).

Another significant difference is that whereas an item in a FORTRAN format statement denotes conversion from a specified internal form (e.g. INTEGER) to a specified external form (e.g. I5), a PL/I format definition only describes the external (printed) form of the item: if need be the actual data item will be coerced into a suitable representation.

A third facet of the difference is the treatment of character strings that are to form part of the output line. FORTRAN is particularly confusing in this respect: if we want a mixed line of output, e.g.

"X = ...   Y = ... "

we have to write something like

WRITE (6, 100) X, Y
FORMAT (4HbX=b, F10.6, 3HY=b, F10.6)

(where b denotes blank). The actual character strings are treated as part of the line format. In PL/I we can specify this much more naturally by

PUT SKIP EDIT ('X=', X, 'Y =', Y), (A, F10.6, A, F10.6)

Here the items to be printed on the line are completely specified within the first bracket, and the second bracket just specifies the format (the 'A' denoting an alphanumeric string). Similar remarks apply to ALGOL 68. Finally we must note the difference in the way that printer spacing is achieved. We have already seen that in FORTRAN each WRITE starts a new line with spacing determined by the first character specified by the FORMAT statement. In addition we can specify that a new line is to start by including an oblique stroke at the appropriate place in the FORMAT statement. Thus line spacing is specified by two differing mechanisms. PL/I improves on this in the sense that spacing associated with the PUT is by means of an explicit qualifier SKIP, PAGE, etc.: line spacing can also be indicated by items in the format list. Only ALGOL 68 adheres strictly to the precept that the format is the sole arbiter of the layout of the printed page. (In the absence of any indication in the format each call of *printf* just carries on where the last one left off.)

In FORTRAN it is possible to include an array name in an input or output list, causing the whole array to be read or written (provided that the associated FORMAT is consistent). However, because FORTRAN perversely stores its arrays in column order this is rarely a useful feature. To permit the printing of an array in row order the "implied DO-loop" has to be introduced. (An explicit DO-loop is no good because each WRITE starts a new line.) Although PL/I stores its arrays in row order and does not forcibly start new lines, the implied DO-loop is still a feature of PL/I I/O – perhaps the designers did not realise why it had to be included in FORTRAN. As we might expect, ALGOL 68 is the most flexible: if *printf* is given an argument of mode **ref** [ ] ... it will print the whole row, and an array can be set out in any desired layout by including print instructions to print slices of the array, controlled by suitable repetition loops.

Methods of specifying formats

The remaining topic to examine is the actual specification of formats for input–output. The classical method, introduced in FORTRAN and followed in PL/I is to use a coded specification, e.g. $Fw.d$ indicates a fixed-point field w characters wide, with d digits after the decimal point. Much to be preferred is the "picture" specification used by ALGOL 68. For example, we might write

$$printf\,(($l\ 10x\ \text{"TOTAL} = \text{"}x\,3zd.2d\$,\ total))$$

The dollar signs delimit the format denotation; this is followed by the variable list, in this case the single item 'total'. The format specifies the following layout.

i)	l	a newline
ii)	$10x$	indent 10 spaces
iii)	"TOTAL = "	print the string TOTAL =
iv)	x	leave one blank
v)	$3zd.2d$	print a number with 3 zero-suppressed

132

digits, one digit, a decimal point and
two trailing digits

In this formal specification, x and l are examples of **positioning** items: other positioning items are p (newpage), y (backspace) and k (tabulation), thus $14k$ in a format specifies a move to character position 14 of the current line. Note that this is an absolute positioning, as compared with $14x$ which is a move of 14 places relative to the current position. It is of interest to note that with the exception of backspace, PL/I provides the same facilities for positioning, since we can include in a format items such as $X(n)$ for a relative move of n places and COLUMN(n) for an absolute move (tab) to column n.

The ALGOL 68 format system provides a number of additional features of interest. A format denotation can include the character 't', which indicates a string of arbitrary length, and an 'a' to stand for a specified number of characters, thus $12a$ would indicate a field of exactly 12 characters. A facility in ALGOL 68 that is not paralleled in any other language is the ability to include choices in a format, in a way analogous to a **case** statement. For example

$$printf\ (\$c(\text{"YES"}, \text{"NO"}, \text{"MAYBE"})\$, n)$$

will print YES, NO or MAYBE according as n has the value 1, 2 or 3. A similar choice facility based on a Boolean value is available:

$$printf\ (\$b(\text{"CR"}, \text{"DR"})\$, balance \geqslant 0)$$

should be self-explanatory.

Miscellaneous facilities in type 1 I/O

However elaborate the formatting facilities provided by a language, there will always be situations where something more is required. When this occurs it is very valuable to be able to do "in-core I/O". By this we mean, taking output as an example, the ability to convert a value into its external representation and store that as a character string in memory. It can then be manipulated using the character handling facilities of the language, and then output as a string. Similar techniques are possible on input. PL/I provides this facility in a neat way. Part of an I/O statement is a file identification: this is usually omitted, since the standard system input and output files are selected by default, but can be explicit, e.g.

GET EDIT FILE(MYFILE) ....

By substituting STRING(S) for the FILE specification, the

named string will be used as the source or destination for the
GET and PUT statements respectively. Indeed, on input a
string expression can be given, thus making available all the
formatting mechanism for string handling. ALGOL 68 provides
similar facilities by means of a number of built-in procedures.
For example,

> *int string* (k, w, r)

converts the integer k into a string of width w characters, the
conversion being done using radix r ($r \leqslant 16$). Similarly

> *real string* (x, w, d, e)

converts the real value x into a string of w characters with d
digits after the decimal point and e digits of exponent. The
inverse procedures *string int* and *string real* are provided,
together with procedures for "fixed-point" conversions.

Type 2 Input/Output

The formal definition of type 2 I/O is that it is a mode of
I/O in which the series of bytes received by the destination
is exactly the same as the series of bytes transmitted by the
source. (If a physical device is involved there may be some
translation imposed by the device: for example a card punch
will translate from the computer's internal code to the actual
punch-card code.) Type 2 I/O transfers records to or from a
file, so before any transfers can take place the attributes and
structure of the file must be defined. In COBOL this is done
in the file section of the DATA DIVISION; in PL/I it can be
done either by DECLAREing the file, when the file is opened,
or by default, or by a combination of all three. In ALGOL 68
it is presumed to be done by job control statements outside
the program.

In PL/I a file for type 2 I/O can have the basic attributes
SEQUENTIAL, SEQUENTIAL KEYED (index sequential) or
DIRECT (KEYED is implied), and READ, WRITE or UPDATE
(i.e. read/write). Once opened, the simple form of I/O for a
sequential file is

> READ
> WRITE   FILE (name) INTO (variable)

For a KEYED file we append

> KEY (expression)

to the statement to select the record to be read; alternatively, we can append

> KEY TO name

where 'name' identifies a character-string variable. In this case
the next record in the file will be read, and its key recorded
as a by-product. In these statements the variable name will be
the name of a structure that matches the file structure. The
type 2 I/O facilities of PL/I reflect strongly the facilities
provided by the S/370 operating system. ALGOL 68 makes
no assumptions about the operating system support of file
structures, and therefore has nothing analogous to SEQUENTIAL
and KEYED attributes. It provides binary transput procedures
that write information in such a way that it can be read again
by the computer, though not by a human reader.

Buffering

Type 2 I/O transfers information in blocks. In some operating
systems double buffering (or more complicated buffering) is
used for transfers to or from serial or sequential files in order
to minimise delays to the program due to waiting for I/O. If
this is the case then for an input transfer a block of information will be transferred from the device to a buffer and later
(when the I/O command is obeyed) from the buffer to the area
named in the I/O instruction. Similar considerations apply,
mutatis mutandis, to an output transfer. If the buffering is done
by the operating system then it is behind the scenes, not under
control of the program, and in PL/I such I/O would be described (confusingly) as UNBUFFERED. However, these transfers
from a buffer to the structure specified by the program (or
vice-versa) represents a possible inefficiency, and PL/I provides
a mechanism for bringing the buffering "into the open" by
specifying the attribute BUFFERED. If this is done we can use
an alternative form of I/O, known as LOCATE mode, in which
the I/O instruction does not specify the source/destination of
a transfer, but uses a pointer to point to the buffer area
currently in use. The form of such a statement on input is

> READ FILE (<*filename*>) SET (<*pointer*>)

When this statement has been obeyed the pointer will point to
the buffer area, so using the associated based variable in the
program will automatically access the current buffer.

For locate-mode output we again use a based variable to
identify the source of the information. In this case the output
area is a based variable with a pointer, and the output is controlled by a LOCATE statement which has the form

LOCATE < *based variable* > FILE (< *filename* >)

LOCATE allocates an output buffer and sets the pointer associated with the based variable accordingly, thus assignments to the based variable in fact cause information to be written into the current buffer. Each time LOCATE is executed it allocates a new buffer and passes the existing buffer to the operating system for output. (The final buffer is passed to the system when the file is CLOSED.)

Exception conditions

In all the discussion of I/O so far, we have not mentioned the possibility of things going wrong. This is surprising, since I/O is one area where the programmer is particularly at risk from forces (and devices) not under his control. It is characteristic of most of the early languages that they expected I/O to proceed without exception conditions arising – which may explain why a datavet program is invariably included in a commercial program suite. The extreme example is Standard Fortran, where it is impossible to find out if an input file has been exhausted, and where an alphabetic character in a field that the FORMAT defines as numeric causes the program to abort. Many nonstandard versions of FORTRAN allow end-of-file detection, e.g.

> READ (5, 100, END = 30) . . .

indicates that control is to go to the statement labelled 30 if the end of file is reached during execution of the statement. The same systems usually allow error trapping, e.g.

> READ (5, 100, END = 30, ERR = 40) . . .

will transfer control to statement label 40 if an error condition arises. However, since the program will not be able to find the nature of the error this is a facility of limited utility. The end-of-file detection is closely analogous to COBOL and PL/I facilities, e.g.

> (COBOL) OPEN MAINFILE AT END PQRS
> (PL/I)   ON ENDFILE DO . . .

(See chapter 8 for an account of PL/I "ON-conditions".)

End of file is only one of several errors that the PL/I programmer can trap. Others are ENDPAGE, which is self-explanatory; CONVERSION, which is an illegal conversion arising during an I/O operation, e.g. presence of a letter in what purports to be a numeric field, and SIZE, which arises if the specified field width is insufficient for the item being printed. It is desirable for the programmer to keep this condition enabled, since if it is disabled PL/I, like some other systems, will merely truncate the field to fit the space available – an act bordering on criminal irresponsibility.

Algol 68 facilities

The facilities provided in Algol 68 for the control of the I/O process are powerful; they are also very complicated, and only an outline is given here. We first have to give some background information about the Algol 68 I/O (or transput) system.

An Algol 68 program communicates with its environment using a set of numbered channels. The correspondence between channels and external devices is assumed to be set up by means of job-control statements outside the program, and will be implementation-dependent. In order to perform input or output (except on the standard channels standin and standout), the programmer declares a variable of mode **file**, and then associates it with a channel by using the open procedure. The file variable is essentially a structure whose fields contain book-keeping information about the channel, e.g. current line number, line width, page size, etc. Certain of the fields are associated with error situations. The most useful fields contain references to procedures, and the general philosophy is that when an error occurs the appropriate procedure for that channel is called. Initially all the relevant fields contain references to system procedures, but the programmer can assign his own procedures if he so wishes. Thus suppose we have a **file** called *myfile*. One of the error situations is logical file end. If the user wishes to deal with this himself he will declare a suitable procedure, *myerrorproc* say, and then assign this by the statement

$$\textit{logical file end } \textbf{of} \textit{ myfile} := \textit{myerrorproc};$$

The error procedures that can be altered in this way are

logical file end	the ultimate and irrevocable end of a file
physical file end	end of line, end of page, or e.g. end of a reel of a multi-reel file
format end	arises if the format is exhausted when there are still items to be processed
value error	arises if the current item does not conform to the format
char error	arises if a character unexpected in context, or totally impossible (e.g. parity error) is encountered

All these procedures are of mode **bool**. When an error occurs the appropriate procedure is called: if it yields false the transput routine carries on with its standard default action, whereas if the error procedure returns true the transput routine assumes that the error has been corrected and proceeds as if nothing untoward had happened. Thus the user can arrange that when physical file ended is called because the end of page has been reached, newpage is called, a heading is output, and by returning the value true the output can proceed. Similarly, if the end of a format is reached the standard action is for the error routine to return false, indicating that the format is to be used again from the beginning. However the user can provide an error routine that will provide an entirely new format and then yield true. All the error procedures except *char error* are parameterless. *Char error* has one parameter of mode **ref char** by which the transput routine communicates the character that it proposes to substitute for the character that provoked the error.

The newcomer to Algol 68 transput is often confused by the fact that in addition to the error mechanisms just described there are also a set of procedures of mode **bool** to interrogate a file variable: they include *logical file ended, file ended, page ended,* and *line ended.* The distinction is that these procedures can be used before a transput operation to determine whether the operation can safely be carried out, whereas the error procedures associated with the file are there to deal with errors that are caught "on the fly". The file-interrogation procedures just mentioned are examples of "environment enquiries". Algol 68 provides a particularly comprehensive set of such procedures. In addition to those quoted, *page number, line number* and *char number* can be used to find the current position at which input or output is taking place: they are all procedures that take a **file** as an argument. Another set of procedures gives information about the available channels. The parameterless procedure *numb channels* gives the number of channels available. The remaining procedures are also parameterless, but deliver a Boolean vector of size 1 .. *nmb channels* that shows which channels have a particular property. Thus *get possible* will show which channels can be read from, *put possible* shows which channels can be written to, *bin possible* shows which channels are available for binary transput and *set possible* shows which channels are random rather than sequential. It is thus possible to construct a very sophisticated I/O package in Algol 68 that will find out for itself all the necessary details of the channels and files to be used.

8

PROGRAM STRUCTURES

I am just going to pray for you at St Paul's,
though with no very lively hope of success.
The Rev Sydney Smith

We have already discussed in Chapter 4 the important concept
of the function or procedure. In this chapter we elaborate
briefly the possible program structures that can be provided in
the framework of a language.

COBOL exemplifies the simplest program structure, being
essentially monolithic. The program is all "on the same level",
with all data being global to the whole program. Two possible
departures from this simple structure are illustrated by FOR-
TRAN and ALGOL 60. A FORTRAN program is made up of
a number of subroutine or function segments that can be
independently compiled: each segment has local data, and in
addition data can be made available to more than one segment
by the use of storage in COMMON blocks. We refer to the
FORTRAN subroutines as *external procedures.* In contrast, an
ALGOL program is a single entity, a block, which can contain
nested inner blocks. We can describe the procedures in ALGOL
60 as *internal* procedures since they are nested within a block.
(Note that we are here referring to static or textual nesting:
in both FORTRAN and ALGOL procedure calls can be nested
dynamically.) PL/I combines the two approaches: a PL/I program is made up of a number of external procedures, each of
which may contain internal procedures nested within it.

Interrupts

It is characteristic of both ALGOL and FORTRAN that procedures are only invoked as a result of an explicit call within
another procedure. There are however other structures that do
not conform to this pattern: the first of these is a structure
that allows for interrupts. Although the interrupt is an important feature of computer hardware, it is rare to find any provision made for it in programming languages: in fact, PL/I is
the only one among the common languages to recognise the
existence of the interrupt. An interrupt is a signal from the
environment external to the part of the program currently

being obeyed. Situations that can cause an interrupt are called CONDITIONS in PL/I: examples are overflow, zero-divide, end of file. (Evidently the actual set of possible conditions is heavily dependent on the operating system and the underlying hardware.) A condition is associated with an action by the statement

ON *<condition>* *<block>*

e.g.

ON ENDFILE GOTO L2;
ON OVERFLOW BEGIN;
    PUT LIST ('OVERFLOW')
    . . . .
    . . . .

The action associated with a condition need not be the same throughout a program, and in particular

ON *<condition>* SYSTEM

will restore standard system action, over-riding any programmer defined action. It should be noted in this connection that the ON statement is an executable statement, not a declaration, thus it is effective from the point at which it is obeyed.

Some conditions in PL/I are always effective: others can be masked out (or disabled). This is done by a condition prefix, e.g.

(OFL NOSIZE): P PROCEDURE

will enable the OVERFLOW condition and disable the SIZE condition within the procedure P. Condition prefixes can be attached to individual statements, giving a very fine degree of control.

The block associated with a condition in an ON statement, the *on-unit*, is treated as an internal procedure, and if the condition arises the on-unit is treated as a procedure called at the point where the interrupt occurred. Control returns either to the instruction that caused the interrupt or to the next statement as appropriate to the cause of the interrupt.

Some ON-conditions correspond to hardware interrupts, others are generated by software. A particularly powerful debugging tool is provided by using this mechanism. This is the CHECK condition. If we prefix a statement (or begin-block) with

(CHECK(*<variable name>*)):

then the CHECK condition is raised whenever the value of that variable is changed. Standard system action is to print the value of the variable: however, by specifying an ON-unit, e.g.

> ON CHECK (<*variable name*>) <*on-unit*> ;

the programmer can take his own action when the value is changed. Thus if we have

> ON CHECK (X, Y) .... ;
> (CHECK (X, Y, Z)): BEGIN , , ,

then whenever the value of X or Y is changed in the BEGIN block the on-unit will be entered. At the end of the ON-unit control reverts to the interrupted program at the next statement. If the value of Z is changed its new value will be printed out as

> Z = *value*

In addition to variable name, the CHECK prefix can specify array names (unsubscripted) and labels; however formal parameters of procedures cannot be CHECKed.

Coroutines

Another program structure to consider is the *coroutine.* The relationship between a calling procedure and the called procedure in a conventional system is asymmetric in two ways. The called procedure is always entered at its head, whereas control reverts to the calling procedure at the point immediately following the call. Furthermore, when the called procedure is entered a new set of local variables is created for it, whereas when control returns to the calling routine the environment is restored to what it was just before the call. In contrast the coroutine relationship is entirely symmetric. If A and B are coroutines, entry to B is always at the point immediately following the most recent call of A by B, and the environment is restored to the state it was in just before the call. Thus A is a subroutine of B, and B is a subroutine of A. Coroutines are very useful for simulating parallel processing and for condensing a two pass process with intermediate storage into a one pass process. They are very rare in programming languages: they appear explicitly in BLISS, and SIMULA provides a facility that is essentially that of coroutines.

Parallel processing

Most languages reflect the conventional single-processor computer architecture. PL/I and ALGOL 68, however, provide for parallel execution of code.

In PL/I there are two variants. The first variant provides for overlapping input–output, by use of an "EVENT" variable. This consists of a flag to signal completion, and an integer code to furnish status information. If we have a simple I/O statement e.g. GET LIST A, B, C then processing of the next statement in the program does not proceed until the input is complete. But if we write

GET LIST EVENT (Z) A, B, C

the next statement will be executed as soon as the input operation has been initiated, and the programmer can regain synchronization by writing WAIT (Z), whose meaning should be obvious. The second variant in PL/I allows a procedure to be called as an autonomous parallel running activity, e.g.

CALL FRED (A, B, C) TASK (T2)

will call the procedure FRED in parallel with the existing program. Again synchronization can be effected by using the WAIT statement.

ALGOL 68 provides for parallel activities synchronized by "Dijkstra" semaphores. There is a mode **sema** (for semaphore) and operators **down** and **up** that correspond to Dijkstra's P and V operations. A special symbol **par** introduces parallel clauses, thus

par begin
　　clause 1, *clause* 2
end

causes clause 1 and clause 2 to be executed in parallel (notionally at least).

It is interesting to note a significant difference between the PL/I and ALGOL 68 approach to parallelism. In the ALGOL 68 example given above, clause 1 and clause 2 are set up as symmetrical sub-tasks and both must complete before the next clause is obeyed. The PL/I system, on the other hand, is asymmetric: the 'parent' task continues after setting up its offspring, and can choose whether or not to WAIT. It should be noted also that the offspring task depends upon the parent for its environment, so it has access to all variables that were in scope when it was set up.

Moreover, if the parent and offspring access common data areas there is no way of guaranteeing that an updating operation by one task will be completed before the other task is allowed to read the information. The Dijkstra semaphores of ALGOL 68 do, of course, provide this protection.

Although ALGOL 68 and PL/I are the only languages to have provision for parallel operation written into their specification, mention should be made of the version of ALGOL 60 provided by Burroughs for use on the B5700 and B6700 series. A procedure may be started as a parallel process by using the basic symbol **process**, thus

> **process** $S(a1, b1, r1, er); S(a2, b2, r2, null)$

will set up two invocations of the procedure S in parallel. The parameter er in the first call of S is a variable of type **event** which can be used to signal completion. Thus the declaration S will have the form

> **procedure** $S(a, b, r, done)$;
> .... ; **event** $done$;
> .... ;
> *cause* $(done)$;
> **end**

and synchronization can be achieved by using the wait primitive, thus

> **process** $S(a1, b1, r1, er)$;
> $S(a2, b2, r2, null)$;
> *wait* (er);

will start two invocations of S and when the second one has finished will test for completion of the first, waiting if necessary.

9

LANGUAGE DESIGN IN ACTION

"You should be glad that bridge fell down –
I was planning to build thirteen more to the
same design"
                    Remark attributed to I. K. Brunel,
                    addressing the Directors of the
                    Great Western Railway.

In this chapter we shall attempt to set out some principles of
language design and illustrate their application by examples
from various languages. The principles set out here may be
regarded as an ideal which very few languages succeed in
achieving. Indeed, some languages show very little evidence of
design: rather, they have just happened. Even these can be
instructive in their own way.

The first requirement of a good language is that its designer(s)
should have a clear idea of what they are trying to achieve:
their aims must be well thought out (and preferably sensible).
Whatever one may say about FORTRAN, the original designers
had very clearly defined objectives, which they achieved success-
fully in the early versions. Regrettably, the same attitude to
design was not shown in any of the extensions, nor was the
design iterated, so that the ANSI standard is essentially a
specification of the behaviour of the early compilers, bugs and
all. (How else can one account for the remarkable rules about
jumping in and out of the extended range of a DO-loop, or
the subtleties of second-level definition?) Clearly seen and
sensible objectives are rare: as a working hypothesis we can
suggest that the probability of achieving them is in inverse
proportion to the number of people involved in the design
process. Thus the best languages are those designed by a single
brilliant individual, or a small coherent group with a dominant
personality. The worst languages are those "designed" by large
committees. (A camel is a horse designed by a committee.)

All design involves compromise, and language design is no
exception. That is why it is important for the designer to have
clearly defined objectives, since without these he cannot judge
when, and how, to compromise. In the case of language design
the designer has two opposing forces. On the one hand he
wants to match his language to what the user wants, and on
the other hand he has to match it to the constraints of the
underlying hardware. Ideally the needs of the user should be
paramount, but although the high-level language exists to shield

the user from the more sordid aspects of the hardware, to conceal entirely the fact that he is dealing with a machine may be to do the user a disservice. As an example, consider simple arithmetic. Pencil-and-paper arithmetic is digital, is decimal (usually), and is carried out with a continually varying number of significant digits. Conversely, except in the case of the integer arithmetic on coded decimal numbers provided on some machines, computer arithmetic is word-oriented: precision is not indefinitely variable, but is in fixed quanta. COBOL and PL/I allow the user to declare fixed point variables of any precision, with a free choice of decimal point, exactly as in pencil-and-paper arithmetic. But because the underlying machine is usually doing binary arithmetic on fixed-length words, PL/I has excessively complicated rules for determining the precision of the result of an operation, and as we have seen in Chapter 3 it is all too easy to get a wrong answer. As an example of erring in the other direction we may take the restrictive rules for subscript expressions in FORTRAN. Here the convenience of the user has been sacrificed in favour of the supposed efficiency of compiling restricted subscript expressions (which may have been the case in the first compiler, but has not been the case since). Here the designers were so obsessed by "efficiency" that they failed to appreciate that most subscript expressions are simple anyway, and provided you can deal with simple cases in an efficient manner there is no need to prohibit complicated cases. What then are the virtues we can look for in a good design?

First, *economy of concepts.* The designer should aim to get the greatest power with the smallest number of concepts. ALGOL 68 is a prime example of success in this direction: the most conspicuous example in the other direction is PL/I.

Secondly, and perhaps most important of all, *uniformity.* No special cases. For example, an integer value may be denoted by an integer constant, or may be computed as the value of an arbitrarily complicated expression, an integer variable being the degenerate (and most common) case. In every context where the language requires an integral value, any of these formulations should be acceptable. Again, ALGOL 68 is an example of virtue in this respect: the counter-example is FORTRAN where the parameters of a DO loop may be integer constants or variables, and array subscripts may be constants, variables, or expressions of a restricted class. Another example of uniformity is that if a language provides both arrays and structures, then it should be possible to have arrays of structures and structures of arrays (ALGOL 68 allows both: ALGOL W does not.) Uniformity makes life easier for the programmer by giving him less to remember. An awful warning in this respect is COBOL, which at first sight appears to be made up entirely of special cases.

Closely allied to the concept of uniformity is the concept of *orthogonality*. Briefly, this means that there should be no inter-action effects between concepts, thus expressions obey the same rule in all contexts (e.g. assignment, subscript, parameter to procedure).

A language that combines all the virtues listed so far will be one in which there exists the possibility of achieving a low error rate in writing programs. Economy of concept and uniformity of application both reduce the likelihood of making mistakes, since there are fewer traps lying in wait for the unwary programmer. A further design choice that is pertinent to this objective is the extent to which consistency checking can be applied at compile time.

Again the extremes are ALGOL 68 and PL/I. It was a design objective of ALGOL 68 that the maximum possible checking should be possible at compile time. Conversely, PL/I deliberately took the view that "anything goes": any syntactically correct sequence of symbols will be accepted, no matter what coercions are involved. We have commented earlier on the $A < B < C$ and $A = B = C$ traps in PL/I. The latter, of course, also illustrates the folly of using one symbol (equals sign) to denote two disparate operations (assignment and testing for equality). Another instructive comparison is the treatment of pointers. In PL/I a pointer can point to anything, and it is easy to get it pointing to rubbish. In ALGOL 68 a pointer is qualified – it is a **ref real** or a **ref proc** or whatever; the use of the **heap** means that a **ref** will rarely point to a meaningless place, and the occasions when a programmer manages to achieve this are detectable by the compiler.

Another aim of the designer should be to protect the user from himself, by making it difficult or impossible for certain kinds of mistake to be made. In general, it is a mistake to provide more than one way of doing the same thing, since the unnecessary choice may confuse the user and make him more error-prone. (A good example is the provision in FORTRAN of both the computed GOTO and the assigned GOTO.) An example of more subtle protection of the user can be seen in the treatment of the equality relation. Most scientific languages define equality for all types of numeric variable, but since the precise equality of two floating-point numbers is nothing more than a fortuitous coincidence, it is arguable that '=' should not be defined for **real** values, unless (as in APL) a "fuzz" is used to convert the relationship into one of approximate equality.

Recognising that mistakes can and will occur, the language

designer should not make it difficult for the error message to be explicit. For example, omitting a DIMENSION statement in FORTRAN will often lead to confusing error messages about statement functions, since function call, array reference and statement function definition all share the same syntax.

All design is a compromise, and one of the most difficult compromises for the language designer is that between permissiveness and protection. Powerful features can be misused: protection can be irksome, and it is not yet clear where the line should be drawn.

We should not leave this subject without a few remarks on FORTRAN and COBOL, since between them they account for most of the world's computing at present. The experienced FORTRAN programmer will usually say that he finds it perfectly satisfactory for his purposes, and doesn't see the need for anything else. (The same remark was probably made about the horse-and-buggy as a means of personal transport at the turn of the century.)

FORTRAN is a very powerful and useful tool. But viewed dispassionately it is a pretty revolting language to use. (The trouble is that, as with parents and their offspring, we are rarely dispassionate in these matters.) FORTRAN is a good example of a pragmatic language: that is to say, the language design is largely dependent on the implementation. This is particularly true of features that have been added subsequent to the original design. Indeed, one can learn a great deal about the early compilers and the machines on which they were implemented by the study of the language. Three examples will suffice: all are features of ANSI FORTRAN.

(i) six character variable names – on the IBM 704 six characters could be packed into a single word.

(ii) restricted form of subscript expressions – it was a design requirement of the original compiler that it should produce efficient code for array references.

(iii) rules on jumping into and out of DO-loops – these are so tortuous that they can only have been derived by trying programs on the machine and seeing what happened.

It is of course deplorable that such historical accidents should have been enshrined in a United States standard. (The Standard has been described as "a loving compilation of all the bugs in the early FORTRAN compilers".)

Although we may criticise FORTRAN (with some justice) we must give it the credit that is due to it as a pioneer. At the time of its conception, "automatic programming" was regarded as a wild innovation, that could never challenge the pre-eminence of the human programmer (or coder). The designers of FORTRAN demonstrated convincingly that it was possible to compile an algebraic language into reasonably efficient code, and made it possible for the scientist and engineer to do his own programming, without calling in the services of a programmer. (Whilst the advantages of having the program written by the man who knows the problem are considerable, it is not an unqualified benefit. Self-taught FORTRAN amateurs have a tendency to proceed with a cavalier disregard for the realities of numerical analysis and numerical approximation, and the accuracy of many of their numerical results must be suspect.) For its time, FORTRAN was a major advance in technology. The remarkable and depressing fact is that it has survived so long with so little alteration, like some hardy weed. This tells us more about the politics and economics of the computer industry than about the merits of the language. In software as in hardware, the predominance of IBM tends to foster an attitude that the way IBM do things must be right: certainly IBM's support for FORTRAN and neglect of ALGOL correlate closely with the acceptance of the languages. (As a counter-example we might consider the fate of PL/I which, despite IBM support, has not prospered in the same way as FORTRAN. This may be due to the fact that the language is excessively complicated, and the early compilers were unbelievably slow. But it is interesting to speculate how PL/I might have fared if IBM had launched it as FORTRAN VI.)

The hold of COBOL on the commercial data-processing world is even greater than that of FORTRAN on the scientific programming world. In this case its pre-eminence is not due to support from IBM but to the policy of the U.S. Government, which at an early stage made the provision of a COBOL compiler a necessary requirement for any computer purchased with Federal funds (an awful warning of the dangers of premature standardisation). The historical development of COBOL shows many parallels with FORTRAN: it demonstrated a viable technique for preparing data processing programs at an early stage in the development of computers, and undoubtedly helped the establishment of the computer as a tool in business. Indeed, for many years it was the only alternative available for commercial data-processing: none of the Algol family (pre-68) were suited to the purpose, and their designers and advocates did a disservice to the cause of language development by not admitting this. The resulting antipathy towards Algol-like languages has caused the commercial world largely to ignore Algol 68, which has everything that is required of a data-processing language. As a result the commercial world remains rooted in the concepts of twenty years ago, metaphorically preferring the rigours of a Dakota to the comfort and convenience of a Boeing 747.

Two particular aspects of COBOL are worth a brief mention. Right from the start, COBOL introduced the concept that the description of the processes could and should be separated from the description of the data being operated on (PROCEDURE DIVISION and DATA DIVISION), and that the logical description of the data could be described separately from its physical characteristics. These are excellent precepts, and it has taken the rest of the programming world a long time to appreciate their virtues. The other aspect is the persistent myth that the English-like form of COBOL makes programs comprehensible. This is nonsense: as a writer in Datamation observed,

> "...we have no evidence that the attempt to simulate English enhances the understandability of programs above the Mickey Mouse level. We have plenty of evidence to the contrary, namely, the whole sorry history of most programming to date..."

It is *structure* that makes programs comprehensible, and structure is precisely what COBOL programs lack.

The design defects of PL/I, and the virtues of ALGOL 68, have been expounded at length already, and need no further elaboration here.

10

SUGGESTIONS FOR FURTHER READING

Guide me, O thou great Redeemer,
Pilgrim through this barren land.
   Cwm Rhondda (Hymns A. & M. No. 196)

The bibliography given in this chapter is by no means exhaustive, but represents a personal selection of texts that the author has read with profit and/or enjoyment.

General books on language and concepts

Higman, B. *A Comparative Study of Programming Languages.* Macdonald/American Elsevier, 1967.
   Unfortunately beginning to show its age, but still well worth reading.

Elson, M. *Concepts of Programming Languages.* Science Research Associates, 1973.
   Gives an interesting alternative account of many of the topics that have been covered in this book.

Sammett, J. E. *Programming Languages: History and Fundamentals.* Prentice-Hall International, 1969.
   A monumental work. Not particularly illuminating on concepts, but an invaluable compendium of information on about 120 languages in use in the U. S. A. at the time of writing. Each language is described and illustrated by a sample program. Particularly good are the historical sections.

Boon, C. (*Editor*) *High Level Languages – Infotech State of the Art Report No. 7.* Infotech Information Ltd., 1972.
   A useful summary of current research areas.

Books on specific languages

ALGOL 60

Dijkstra, E. W. *A Primer of Algol 60 Programming.* Academic Press, 1962.
   An elegant and concise treatment by the master.

Froberg, C. E. and Eckman, T. *Introduction to Algol Programming.* Studentlitteratur, Sweden, 1965. (Distributed by

Petrocelli, New York).
This is an excellent textbook.

ALGOL 68
Woodward, P. and Bond, S. G. *Algol 68-R Users Handbook.* HMSO, London, 1974. (Second edition)
A splendid introduction.

Lindsay, C. and van der Meulen, S. G. *Informal Introduction to Algol 68.* North Holland, 1971.
Comes with the imprimatur of IFIP. Comprehensive and readable.

APL
Gilman, L. and Rose, A. J. *APL – an interactive approach.* Wiley, 1970.

BASIC
Kemeny, J. G. and Kurtz, T. E. *BASIC Programming.* Wiley, 1971. (Second edition)
The original, and still the best.

COBOL
Lysegard, A. *Introduction to COBOL.* Studentlitteratur, Sweden, 1968 (Distributed by Petrocelli, New York).
An excellent introduction.

Stuart, F. *Introduction to Standard COBOL Programming.* Harcourt, Brace Jovanovitch, 1974.
Another very clear text.

FORTRAN
Organick, E. and Meissner, L. *FORTRAN IV Second Edition.* Addison Wesley, 1975.
A good comprehensive coverage. Make sure you get the second edition, which at the time of writing is only published in the U. S. A., and does not appear in the British catalogues.

Anon. *Standard Fortran Programming Manual.* National Computer Centre, 1970.
Will probably tell you more about FORTRAN than you wish to know.

LISP
Weissman, C. *LISP 1.5 Primer.* Dickenson, 1967.
If anyone can guide you through the intricacies of LISP, Weissman will do it.

PASCAL
Jensen, K. and Wirth, N. *User Guide and Report.* Springer-Verlag, 1975.

The only book on PASCAL, written with authority and clarity.

PL/I

Bohl, M. and Walter, A. *Introduction to PL/I Programming and PL/C.* Science Research Associates, 1973.
An excellent text.

Neuhold, E. J. and Lawson, H. W. *The PL/I Machine: an introduction to programming.* Addison Wesley, 1971.
A more thorough coverage of a smaller range of topics.

POP-2

Burstall, R. M., Collins, J. S. and Popplestone, R. J. *Programming in POP-2.* Edinburgh University Press, 1971.

SIMULA

Birtwistle, G. M., Dahl, O-J., Myrhaug, B. and Nygaard, K. *SIMULA BEGIN.* Auerbach, 1975.
The only book on SIMULA. Fortunately it is very good.

SNOBOL

Griswold, R. F. and Griswold, M. T. *A SNOBOL 4 Primer.* Prentice-Hall, 1973.

Griswold, R. E., Poage, J. F. and Polonsky, I. P. *The SNOBOL 4 Programming Language.* Prentice-Hall, 1968.
Griswold is the "father" of SNOBOL, and describes it with enthusiasm and clarity.

Miscellaneous Topics

Humby, E. *Programs from Decision Tables.* Macdonald/ American Elsevier, 1973.
A good account of a generally-neglected way of writing programs.

Kernighan, B. W. and Plauger, P. J. *The Elements of Programming Style.* McGraw Hill, 1974.
Shows how language features can be exploited, and also how they can be misused.

Weinberg, G. M. *The Psychology of Computer Programming.* Van Nostrand Rheinhold, 1971.
A thoughtful and thought-provoking study of programming as a human activity. Essential reading for anyone interested in the subject.

11

EXERCISES

And moreover, because the preacher was wise, he still
taught the people knowledge; yea, he gave good heed,
and sought out, and set in order many proverbs,
Ecclesiastes, XII, v. 9

The exercises that follow are taken from the degree examinations of various U. K. universities, each question being individually attributed.

1. Write brief notes on the following features of the
FORTRAN IV language:
   (a)   Implicit types
   (b)   Statement functions
   (c)   Implied DO-loops
   (d)   The EXTERNAL statement
   (e)   The EQUIVALENCE statement

(St Andrews, 1974)

2. What is a meta language? Describe briefly the meta language
of COBOL and compare it with that of ALGOL.
   Describe the DATA DIVISION of the COBOL language
giving special attention to editing and the use of COMPUTA-
TIONAL. Indicate the contribution made by COBOL to the
technology of programming languages.

(City University B. Sc., 1971)

3. Describe briefly why the COBOL language is more appropriate for Data Processing applications of computers than an
algebraic language such as Algol W. Illustrate the points you
make with examples. Explain briefly the purpose of the four
divisions of a COBOL program, and suggest reasons why the
COBOL language has been designed in this way.
   Explain what is meant by the term CONDITION NAME in
COBOL. Give an example showing how a condition name
would be defined, and how it would subsequently be used.

(Newcastle B. Sc., 1972)

4. What are the most significant differences between the Algol W and APL languages with respect to ease of programming, and clarity of programs?

(Newcastle M. Sc., 1972)

5. It has been stated that the aims of the designers of the COBOL language were to produce a programming language which provided (among other advantages): readability of programs, portability of programs, separation of data and program and the hierarchical structuring of data.

Give examples from the language of the ways in which COBOL has attempted to achieve these aims, and discuss whether or not the attempts have been successful.

(Newcastle B. Sc., 1975)

6. What concepts seem useful in describing programming languages? What criteria should be used in judging the design of a programming language?

Compare some languages, for example, Algol 60, Lisp 1.5, Snobol 4, Simula 67.
- (a) Attempt to describe them in terms of your suggested concepts.
- (b) Criticise them according to your suggested criteria.

(Queen Mary College B. Sc., 1971)

7. Discuss some different types of control structure that are provided in programming languages, including iteration, subroutines, monitoring, coroutines and parallel processes. To what extent can the various types of control be expressed by scheduling relations over sequential processes?

(Queen Mary College B. Sc., 1971)

8. Compare the structures of Algol W and Fortran IV, so far as they influence the accessibility of storage and labels defined in one part of a program from statements in another part.

(St Andrews, 1972)

9. Describe, giving examples, the following features of Algol W:
- (a) the **if** statement
- (b) **bit** sequences and the operators which act on them
- (c) the declaration of **arrays**

154

(d) the use of **arrays** as formal parameters of **procedures**.

(St Andrews, 1972)

10. Give short answers comparing and contrasting FORTRAN and ALGOL W for any four of the following language features.
  (i) Scope of identifiers.
  (ii) Procedures, functions, subroutines.
  (iii) Data Structures (i.e. arrays, lists, etc.).
  (iv) Data types, names and declarations.
  (v) Control of loops.
  (vi) Input and Output.
In each case give examples drawn from both programming languages.

(Newcastle B. Sc., 1975)

11. Programming languages A and B both have the syntax of ALGOL 60 and differ only in the way identifiers are bound to values. The binding of identifiers in these languages can be explained by the following rules, which assume an interpretation scheme based upon the creation of a new activation record upon entry to each block or procedure:
  (A) The value of an identifier in language A is determined by searching the current activation record for a matching name. If a match is found, the associated value is used; otherwise the search continues through successive activation records on the static link chain.
  (B) The value of an identifier in language B is determined by a similar search, but the dynamic link chain is followed at each step.
For the purposes of this explanation, each activation record is assumed to include an entry containing the name and value of each local variable.
  (1) Which language is, in fact, ALGOL 60?
  (2) Consider the following program, in which "write" identifies a standard output procedure:

```
begin integer a, b, c;
  procedure P;
    begin
    b := c := b + 1; write (a); write (c)
    end P;
  procedure Q;
    begin integer a, b;
    a := b := 3; P
    end Q;
  a := b := c := 1; P; Q
end
```

What output does this produce as a language A program? As a language B program?

(3) Assume that these two languages are to be implemented on a conventional digital computer with a set of base or index registers. For each language, outline a scheme for accessing variables in the object code. What associated book-keeping operations are required upon block/procedure entry and exit? Comment upon the relative efficiencies of the schemes you have chosen.

(Newcastle M. Sc., 1972)

12. Discuss two methods which can be used in a programming language to protect particular variables from undesired side effects. For each method show the linguistic constructions which are needed, giving a precise account of their meaning and examples of their use.

(St Andrews, 1974)

13. (a) Explain briefly what is meant by "local" and "global" identifiers in ALGOL W. What is the "scope" of an identifier? Illustrate, by writing a short program, how an identifier may be declared in a block enclosing a given block but be inaccessible within the given block. Consider the following ALGOL W program

```
1.    BEGIN
2.       INTEGER N;
3.       READ(N);
4.       BEGIN
5.          INTEGER ARRAY B(1 : : N);
6.          INTEGER K, J;
7.          FOR K := 1 UNTIL N DO B(K) := K;
8.          K := 2;
9.          WHILE K < = SQRT(N) DO
10.         BEGIN
11.            IF B(K)¬= 0 THEN
12.            BEGIN
13.               J := K * K;
14.               WHILE J < = N DO
15.               BEGIN
16.                  B(J) := 0; J := J + K;
17.               END
18.            END
19.            K := K + 1;
20.         END;
```

156

```
21.      FOR K := 1 UNTIL N DO
22.    END;

22.          IF B(K) ⌐= 0 THEN WRITEON(B(K))
23.       END
24.    END.
```

(b) What is the scope of the variable N, declared in line 2, and the variables K and J, declared in line 6? Why is it necessary to introduce the block which starts at line 4?

(c) What output would result from the program if the data card contained the value 20? Deduce what output the program will produce for general values of N.

(Newcastle B. Sc., 1975)

14. Describe the syntax and semantics of the Algol W iterative statements **for** and **while**. Compare their uses giving short examples.

(St Andrews, 1974)

15. Describe the rules governing the use of arrays as parameters to procedures in Algol W.

Design a procedure which will add together two single subscript real arrays element by element, placing the sum values in a third single subscript real array. Show how this procedure can be used to add together two rows from a double subscript array. Would any problems be presented if the result of this addition were placed in a column of the same array?

This ability to slice arrays in Algol W can be simulated using name parameters (so called Jensen's device). What are the advantages and disadvantages of doing this?

(Newcastle M. Sc., 1975)

16. Describe informally the following features of Algol W. Give an example of each.

(a)   FOR STEP UNTIL DO loops.

(b)   The methods of call for the parameters of procedures.

(c)   The string variables and functions.

(St Andrews, 1972)

17. Explain what is meant by the term *recursion* used in connection with computer programs.

Describe the action of the following procedure.

procedure *convert_to_binary* (**integer value** *n*);
if *n* ≠ 0 **then**
    begin
    convert_to_binary (*n* **div** 2);
    writeon (*I_W* := 1; *n* **rem** 2)
    end *convert_to_binary*

Generalise this procedure to convert to the representation of
the number *n* to any base. The base should be specified as
a parameter.

(St Andrews, 1974)

18. Compare and contrast the run-time storage allocation
procedures required for FORTRAN and ALGOL 60. Illustrate
your answer by considering what run-time storage actions are
required to
    (a)   read a variable length vector
and
    (b)   call a function subroutine
in each language. Why is run-time storage allocation for
ALGOL W more complex than that for ALGOL 60? Suggest
a technique which might be used to solve the problem.

(St Andrews, 1974)

19. What do we mean by an 'efficient program'? Discuss the
advantages and disadvantages of using BASED storage allocation in PL/I with respect to efficiency.
    What is a 'side-effect'? Give two program examples illustrating
side-effect situations, preferably in Algol 60.

(Imperial College M. Sc., 1973)

20. (a) Describe the interrupt facilities offered by PL/I. Discuss
        how they can influence program implementation.
    (b) Compare and contrast the concepts of program structure
        in Algol and Fortran.

(Imperial College M. Sc., 1973)

21. Describe how simple type parameters in Algol W can be
further specified with value or result and define precisely the
four parameter mechanisms which are so obtained.

(Newcastle B. Sc., 1974)

22. Explain what is meant by the terms
   (i) call-by-value
   (ii) call-by-reference
   (iii) call-by-substitution
when applied to the implementation of the actual/formal correspondence of parameters.

   Discuss the relative efficiency of each.

   Define the term "side-effect". Give examples showing side-effect differences between the above three implementations.

(St Andrews, 1974)

23. You are provided with the following two Algol "type" procedures:
   real procedure *multiassign* (a, b, c); **value** b; **real** a, b, c;
   begin $c := a$; *multiassign* $:= 1.0$; **end** *multiassign*;
   real procedure *Jensen* (i, j, k, l, m, n); **value** j, k, l;
   integer i, j, k, l; **real** m, n;
   begin for $i := j$ **step** k **until** l **do** $n := m$; *Jensen* $:= 1.0$;
   end *Jensen*;

   Write a procedure call for *Jensen* $(...)$ which will calculate the matrix product C of the compatible matrices A and B. (A, B and C are declared in a declaration array $A[1:p, 1:q]$, $B[1:q, 1:r]$, $C[1:p, 1:r]$;.) You are to assume that the elements of A and B are correctly in place and the elements of C are undefined. The procedure call of *Jensen* $(...)$ may include further calls of *Jensen* and *multiassign* in its parameters, but no other procedures should be used. The resulting procedure call should form a single Algol statement to evaluate the matrix product $A.B = C$.

(Glasgow B. Sc., 1970)

24. Describe and compare the parameter-passing methods available in Algol W, Pascal and one of the following: APL, Fortran, PL/I. Give examples to show the effects of each of these methods when a variable is accessed by a procedure activation both via a parameter and as a non-local variable. Also, describe the effects of passing one variable to a procedure in two formal parameter positions in the same call.

(Glasgow B. Sc., 1975)

25. Describe the record and string handling facilities of Algol W, pointing out any defects, and give examples of better

methods available in other programming languages.

(Glasgow B. Sc., 1974)

26. Describe in detail the data structures of Algol 60, and the limitations these impose on the types of problem for which Algol 60 can be used. What extensions to the language would you consider desirable to meet these limitations?

Describe a high-level language with a different form of data structure, indicating the reasons for the choice of this structure and its uses.

(Glasgow B. Sc., 1970)

27. What is a data structure; a data structure type?

How can user defined data structure types be represented and how can these representations be specified in a programming language?

What are the limitations of the specification mechanisms currently known?

How are these specifications used in programming?

(Queen Mary College B. Sc., 1971)

GENERAL INDEX

Topics related to specific languages
will be found in the Index of
Languages on page 163

actual parameters, 53
anonymous values, 31
array dimensionality, 86
   rank, 86
   references, syntactic form of, 89
   slices, 90
   storage, 86
arrays, abstract model of, 97
   anonymous, 91
   constant, 93
   in functions and procedures, 94
   non-connected, 103
assessment of COBOL design, 147
assessment of FORTRAN design, 147
assignment collateral, 42
   command, 41
   multiple, 41
attributes of functions and
      procedures, 64

bit strings, 121
Boolean expressions, 47
   variables, 19
buffered I/O, 135

call by name, 60 ff
call by value, 56
case statement, 48
chain, dynamic, 67
   static, 67
classification of languages, 9 ff
commands, 34
comments, 6, 7
complete arrays, operations on, 91
compound commands, 34
conditional command, 44
control and sequencing, 42
control transfer, 50
coroutines, 141
correctness, virtues of, 8

dangling else, 44
data attributes, 16
declarations, 20
   constant, 22
   initialised, 22
de-referencing, 36
design criteria, 144 ff
display, 67

expression evaluation, 35
expressions, 33
   mixed mode, 37 ff
   mixed precision, 39
exception conditions in I/O, 136, 138
external form, 4
   surprising consequences of
      Algol 60 rules, 5

file attributes, 125, 134
for statement, 49
formal parameters, 53
FORMAT specification, 130
   in ALGOL 68, 132, 137
functions, 53 ff
   anonymous, 80
   as data objects, 79
   generic, 71

GOTO statement, 51

interrupts, 139
I/O, 124 ff
   in ALGOL 68, 129
   in FORTRAN, 126
   in PL/I, 127

lambda expressions, 80
language as a vehicle of
      communication, 3
left-hand functions, 77

INDEX OF LANGUAGES

PL/I

ALLOCATEd storage, 21, 111
arrays, complete, operations on, 91, 92
    dangers of, 92
array declaration, 103
arrays, non-connected, 103
BASED storage, 111
bit string operations, 122
Boolean expressions, poor substitute for, 47
Boolean variables, 19
    traps for the unwary, 19, 20
break character, 6
comments, 6, 7
compound statements, 34
condemnation of design aims, 145 ff
conditional statement, 45
CONTROLLED storage, 111
dangling else, inelegant resolution of, 45
data attributes, 22
declarations, danger of, 27
    implicit, 26
DO, confusing use of, 34
DO loop, 50
file attributes, 134
fixed point precision, unanticipated consequences of allowing choice, 39, 40
floating point, illusory freedom of choice in choosing precision, 18
function values, restrictions on, 55
generic functions, 71
interrupts, unique recognition of, 140
I/O, 127
    exception conditions, 136
    formats, 131
LOCATE mode I/O, 135
mixed mode expressions, surprising liberality of, 37
multiple assignment, 42
    disastrous consequences of wrong notation, 42
name, fully qualified, 102
naming of structure elements, 101
ON conditions, 140
parameter passing, 60
PICTURE, 117
POINTER, 110
    confusing notation for, 111
procedure heading, 65
pseudo-variables, 77
reserved words, non-existence of, 6

STATIC storage as substitute for own, 67
    as substitute for COMMON, 68
storage modes, 29, 30
string declaration, 117
string operations, built-in functions for, 118, 119
structure assignment BY NAME, 107
TASKing, 142

POP-2

anonymous variables, 31
Boolean expressions and operators, 47
dangling else, resolution of, 44
declarations, 20
function variables, 79
lambda expressions, 80
left-hand functions, 77
operator definition, 75
partial application, 69
postfix notation, virtues of, 72
stack, explicit, 31
structures, 106 ff

SNOBOL 4

intelligent treatment of quotes, 7
string manipulations in, 120 ff